Contagious Faith

EMPOWERING STUDENT LEADERSHIP IN YOUTH EVANGELISM

by
Dave Rahn and Terry Linhart

Group
Loveland, Colorado

Dedication

This book is dedicated to Christian men and women around the world who dedicate themselves each morning to make a difference in the lives of teenagers. They often receive little applause or recognition, but they press on, trying to be increasingly faithful to the one who's called them to the exciting, and sometimes frustrating, task of being an effective youth worker.

Contagious Faith

Copyright © 2000 Dave Rahn and Terry Linhart

Visit our Web site: **www.grouppublishing.com**

Credits
Editor: Amy Simpson
Creative Development Editor: Jim Kochenburger
Chief Creative Officer: Joani Schultz
Copy Editor: Dena Twinem
Art Director: Kari K. Monson
Cover Art Director: Jeff A. Storm
Cover Designer: Alan Furst Inc.
Computer Graphic Artists: Andrea Reider and Tracy K. Donaldson
Production Manager: Alexander Jorgensen

Library of Congress Cataloging-in-Publication Data
Rahn, Dave, 1954-
   Contagious faith : empowering student leadership in youth evangelism / by Dave Rahn
and Terry Linhart.
     p. cm.
   ISBN 0-7644-2194-8 (alk. paper)
   1. Peer-group church work with youth. 2. Church work with students. 3. Evangelistic
work. I. Linhart, Terry, 1964- II. Title.

BV4447 .R34 2000
259'.23--dc21

                                                 00-037563

10 9 8 7 6 5 4 3 2 1   09 08 07 06 05 04 03 02 01 00

Printed in the United States of America.

Acknowledgments

There is a boatload of people without whom we couldn't have done the research or writing to bring this project to completion. First of all, we want to thank those churches, organizations, and youth workers who participated in our study. May their vulnerability and willingness to be "under the spotlight" be the seeds for a continued rich blessing. In alphabetical order, here they are:

Mike Allen at Grace Chapel in Boston, Massachusetts

Keith Ancar at Santa Clara Youth for Christ, Santa Clara, California

Scott Benson at Winnetka Bible Church in Winnetka, Illinois

Rick Cavitt at Coggin Avenue Baptist Church in Brownwood, Texas

Johnny Derouen at Travis Avenue Baptist Church in Fort Worth, Texas

Charlie Dodd at First Baptist Church in Midland, Texas

Bill Duppenthaller at Gig Harbor Young Life in Gig Harbor, Washington

Brian Hook at Grace Community Church in Detroit, Michigan

Marvin Jacobo at First Baptist Church in Modesto, California

Brad Johnson at Carroll Campus Life in Fort Wayne, Indiana

Chris Kainu at Summitview Community Church in Vancouver, Washington

Keith Krueger at Faith Evangelical Free Church in Milford, Ohio

Al Mellinger at MacPherson Free Methodist Church in MacPherson, Kansas

Don Nixon at Metro Pittsburgh Youth for Christ, Pittsburgh, Pennsylvania

Ed Noble at Evangelical Free Church of Fresno in Fresno, California

Todd Rodarmel at Coast Hills Community Church in Aliso Viejo, California

Pete Spear at McKinney Memorial Bible Church in Fort Worth, Texas

Larry Stair at Grace Church of Arvada in Arvada, Colorado

Roger Vezeau at College Park United Brethren Church in Huntington, Indiana

Corey Webb at Alamo City Fellowship in San Antonio, Texas

Dan Weyerhauser at Lakeland Evangelical Free Church in Grayslake, Illinois

Rob Yonan at Wheaton First Baptist Church in Wheaton, Illinois

Thanks to our wives, Susie Rahn and Kelly Linhart, and our families for encouraging us as we traveled, researched, worried, and wrote. Your patience and love is treasured.

Thanks to Huntington College and Hope Missionary Church for their support and understanding of us. It's great to be empowered to chase dreams!

We want to express our deepest appreciation to the MacLeod Foundation for the two generous grants that funded the travel, making it possible to conduct this research project.

Thanks to the undergraduates who phoned, traveled to, and conducted the majority of inquiries, interviews, and data collection: Ben Hamm, Christy Miller, David Ramseyer, Kathy Houk, Israel Rodriguez, Jeremy McClung, Mindy Wier, Trisha Springer, Michelle Slemons, and Chuck Fenwick. You helped us keep our perspective.

Thanks to Mrs. Carol Lister, Charity Coffey, and Kristi Horner for their help in compiling statistics, mailing surveys, and keeping the project organized.

Thanks to Dr. Karen Jones for her support and encouragement throughout this project.

Thanks to Linda Honegger for flying the team to our final visit. What a way to finish!

Thanks to Stoller's Travel and Tours for the help in arranging travel and finding inexpensive flights.

Thanks to Keith Koteskey for his insightful help with the manuscript.

Thanks to Rick Lawrence, Amy Simpson, and the entire Group staff for their commitment to this project and their help in shaping this book.

Finally, thanks to all the student leaders with whom we have served through the years. Your lives have inspired us. They still do.

Contents

Foreword

KEVIN HARLAN, *Chief of Staff*

Fellowship of Christian Athletes

Several years ago, a group of key FCA leaders met together with two leaders outside FCA (Barry St. Clair and Bruce Johnson) to discuss our Huddle strategy, FCA's campus ministry strategy for junior high schools, senior high schools, and colleges. It was clear that God was alive and active on campuses across the country as our numbers were growing at a rapid pace; however, we wanted to get together and discuss the issue of quality of ministry and what the future held for us.

During our time together, we did what you do during planning sessions: We began writing on flip charts. (I think it's a therapeutic exercise. You write real big and it makes you feel as if you're getting a lot done!) During that time, while doing a simple SWOT analysis (strengths/weaknesses/opportunities/threats), something emerged and caught us all by surprise. A similar item appeared on both our "opportunity" page and our "threat" page—it was the diminishing opportunity for adults to be involved in hands-on campus ministry, and the requirement for students to lead.

Because equal access legislation required schools' clubs to be student-initiated and student-led, it was becoming more difficult for an adult to be involved, and muddy as to the role of the adult. That was the threat. However, as we discussed this subject, we all realized that if we were to design a strategy that would be most effective to reach a campus for Christ, it would be through a team of students who were working together as leaders to see it happen. It was a blessing and a curse at the same time.

As an organization, we have always believed in the value of student leadership, and since the beginning of our Huddle strategy over thirty years ago, we have had students serving as "officers" of the Huddle. However, something special happened in my mind that day. I began to view student leaders as central to the strategy, not simply a group of people to help the adults carry out the ministry. I truly believe that God wants to reach this generation through the testimonies of this generation, and the campus ministry strategy of students leading with adults walking along with them is a powerful vehicle.

That's what excites me most about this book. Dave and Terry have captured the key components of successful student leadership, and they've given us all a model to follow. The principles and strategies they outline not only have the statistical research to support them, but are practical and can be implemented where you serve. Let me give you one example of how I know this to be true.

Dave recently attended our FCA Leadership Institute and talked through the findings he and Terry had discovered as well as their conclusions. It was a stimulating discussion with our class of twenty-four leaders, and it was obvious that he had hit a passion with our staff. The dialogue continued through the meal and after he left. A few months later, the P.I.T. Crew strategy, which you will find outlined in this book, emerged in FCA with an implementation plan. Our leaders were actively pursuing ways to help our student leaders engage in prayer, and we're testing the model now in one of our regions. You can see what we've done on our Web site—www.fca.org. It's one practical expression of the principles you'll find in this book.

As people who work with students, we are living in an exciting time. We have a generation emerging who is eager to do evangelism among their peers and who is hungry for tools and people to help them. May we make the most of this opportunity, seize this moment in time, and do all we can to equip students to share the life-changing message of the gospel of Christ.

INTRODUCTION:
The Research Behind the Book

What if you could travel the country, uncovering rich truths in an area of ministry important to you? Better yet, what if you could take students with you and enrich their learning as you visited hotbeds of youth ministry effectiveness? That was the joy of our project. After Dave initially invited Terry to join him in the research, the study you will read about in this book ended up becoming Terry's culmination project for his master's degree at Huntington College's Graduate School of Christian Ministries. It also was a great experience for ten undergraduates in the educational and youth ministry programs at Huntington College.

This research project has produced a rare glimpse inside some of the hottest youth groups in America where peer evangelism has been common. Our research endeavor began in the fall of 1996 when we began to surface the names of youth ministries where peer evangelism was known to be strong. Two questions guided our search: (1) What are the differences between student leaders who reach their friends for Christ and those who don't? and (2) What are the common factors in youth ministries where teenagers reaching teenagers for Christ is the norm?

To find these ministries, we asked denominational youth leaders, youth directors, youth ministry educators, writers, and parachurch youth ministry leaders to nominate ministry sites for our consideration. The requests for nominations came via e-mail and phone conversations, seminars and conferences, and in group settings as well as individual settings. After four months of such efforts, 109 different youth ministries across the United States had been suggested for our research. This relatively small population represented a limitation of this study that we were aware of when we started the project.

On the other hand, it was the first insight we had into the true state of student-leadership effectiveness. There aren't a lot of people who have had a history of doing student leadership well.

We then selected a team of ten undergraduates in the educational and youth ministry departments from Huntington College for participation in the project, allowing them the opportunity to travel around the country and get firsthand insight regarding these ministries. The MacLeod Foundation generously supplied two different grants for the travel expenses related to the research.

Our next task was to determine which of the 109 nominated youth ministries met our criteria for effective student leadership. We divided them among the team members so we could conduct phone interviews, which helped us determine if they fit the profile of the kind of group we were interested in studying. We had decided to focus on learning from those groups that had a *history* of student leader effectiveness. Team members made contact with the youth leaders and requested twenty-minute phone appointments so we could ask questions about the roles of student leaders in their ministries. Our intent was to determine which of the nominated youth ministry sites met our standard of demonstrating three or more years where peer-to-peer evangelism was common.

When a team member completed his or her phone interview, he or she assigned the ministry to one of three categories. The first category (A) represented those that deserved serious consideration for our study. The second group (B) included those who might be worth a closer look, but there were some questions about fit. The last category (C) represented those who clearly did not fit the profile we were looking for, were unwilling to help, or may have been in a significant leadership transition.

Our strategy was to visit as many A sites as possible around the country, given the limitations of our budget and time. We decided that we could see as many as twenty sites between March and May of 1997. Logistical complications led us to reduce our site visits to seventeen that year.

When visiting a location, usually in teams of two or more, team members used three data-gathering devices. These distinct differences in our data collection not only allowed us to gather statistics, but to use qualitative methods in our inquiry as well. The first approach could give us *breadth* of knowledge, but we relied on the second and third to supply us with *depth* of insight.

All students filled out a forced-choice survey answering eight questions about themselves and then twenty-four questions about different evangelism-related behaviors. For each of these items, student responses gave indication on a Likert-like scale of the *frequency* with which they engaged in specific behaviors.

Team members then divided the student leaders into small groups for "timed team responses." Adult volunteers formed separate groups while the youth leader filled out a response form independently. Team members gave each small group the same question to answer and asked group members to agree on the top three answers for that question regarding their ministry. We strictly enforced a five-minute time limit for each question. Our intent was to surface commonly agreed-upon elements in the life of each particular youth ministry in a way that would allow us some control concerning peer influence during discussion. When we checked the various responses against each other, we were pleased with how this method helped us to see not just what particular small groups believed, but what an entire student leadership team thought was significant.

Finally, we used a large-group discussion that helped us discover the spirit, expectations, and "personality" of the group. We took extensive notes during these discussions, and you will see some of the quotes we picked up woven throughout the book. Youth leaders also supplied us with descriptive statistics (numbers of kids, volunteers, and so on) regarding the youth ministry.

After we concluded the visits, we spent the summer of 1997 engaging in analytical work and hypothesis development. We formulated eight preliminary conclusions, gaining agreement on their validity among members of the research team. As interesting as our findings were, we concluded that if we could further explore some of our tentative conclusions with additional research, our study would be significantly strengthened. The second funding grant from the MacLeod Foundation made it possible to expand our research another year.

In the second year of study we pared down the undergraduate team to four students and developed on-site strategies that would help us check the hypotheses. In addition to using the previous year's three data-gathering strategies, we developed an individual interview template and used it with student leaders at each location. We also altered the large-group discussion questions to help us uncover specific aspects of the youth ministries' histories, aiding us particularly as we checked out our "stages of vitality" hypotheses (see chapter 7).

As we decided where we wanted to go with our research, we approached some major evangelism organizations and asked them to give us the names of youth ministries that represented the "best stuff" of their ministry approaches. We wanted as diverse a project as possible. We visited seven sites between October 1997 and March 1998; two of them were revisits of locations from our first year.

In total, 424 high school students from twenty-two different youth ministries participated in our study. They came from student leadership teams ranging in size from six to fifty-one and represented youth ministries with official rolls from 80 to 850. Attendance at the largest weekly events for these groups ranged from 35 to 350.

The result of the visits is a fertile combination of statistics, small-group reports, observations, adult staff and youth pastor interviews, and detailed one-on-one interviews. Our central focus was on the heroes of the research, student leaders who take uncommonly bold steps to reach their peers for Jesus Christ.

This project would not have been possible without the willingness and warmth of local youth leaders who gave time, hospitality, and access to their students in allowing us to visit and conduct the research. With a clear commitment to kingdom values, their openness and humility make it possible for all of us to be more faithful in our ministry efforts. Some have moved on to other ministries, but many are still at these same locations, serving Jesus with honor, perseverance, and diligence. May God use this book to multiply their numbers!

Foundational Issues in Student Leadership

CHAPTER 1:
The Evangelism Vision of Student Leadership

Joel wrote his own manual to guide an expansive citywide prayer movement among high-school students in his city. Melissa's tender heart, sensitive spirit, and enthusiastic energy invigorated her church's effective youth worship services. In a small rural community, Sheri decided to organize a campus Bible club at her school, stepping into the wide-open leadership vacuum that has never attracted consistent, adult-led youth ministry to her home territory. Kenny assumed his teaching role in the new youth church almost naturally, functioning as a seventeen-year-old elder among his peers. Pat served two consecutive terms as the elected youth representative to her church's board of administration.

Calling these students "leaders" seems like a no-brainer. But we're not convinced that everyone always means the same thing when they use the word "leader."

Some youth workers would sooner give up their favorite T-shirts than compromise on what they mean by "student leadership." When they come to the fork in the road where definitions head off in different directions, they choose to head down the path of leadership-as-influence. By doing so, they disagree with the notion that leadership needs to be attached to position or status within a formal organizational framework. Joel, Melissa, Kenny, and even Sheri all *emerged* as leaders, and the organizational structure was simply a handy context in which they could flex their gifts for peer influence. On the other hand, Pat's leadership is exclusively tied to the formal position she holds in the church.

We think this definition distinction is important to clarify right up front in a book about student leadership. Readers have a right to know what *we mean* by the term. While this book is built upon research findings that help us understand a lot of the *how* questions related to effective student leadership, one of the main reasons for Link Institute's

14

National Student Leadership Research Project was to champion a definition of student leaders that includes peer evangelism. By doing so, we align ourselves with those who see leadership as influence. (Huntington College's Link Institute is an organization dedicated to faithful and effective youth ministry.)

With two different travel-funding grants from the MacLeod Foundation, our team conducted a two-year inquiry that led us to visit some of the most exciting youth ministries in the country. We visited more than twenty different locations; collected survey data from more than four hundred student leaders; conducted large-group, small-group, and individual interviews…all to discover the common factors present in those youth ministries that historically have demonstrated they can mobilize students for a ministry of outreach to their peers. The definition of student leaders we'll develop in this chapter helped us screen sites for our study. At the end of the chapter we'll clue you in about where we're headed as we discuss the practical implications of what we discovered.

But for now we'd like to make the case for rooting our definition of student leadership in the middle of interpersonal influence.

Student Leadership as Influence

Veteran youth workers don't have trouble agreeing that natural social pressures characterize the nonformal world of young people, where friends wield escalating influence on one another. Students sample their first beer or experiment sexually when their friends support such adventures. Adolescents—at least for a time—tend to be more influenced by their closest friends than by TV, music, sports, education, and even family. This is bad news for those who think funding elaborate institutional programs will bring about lasting change, but it plays wonderfully into our Lord's master design for character transformation. Every Christian is called to flavor his or her peer culture with Christ-salt, to be the Jesus light-shafts their friends need. Students who intentionally build bridges of love to their friends will find ever-expanding opportunities to influence in Jesus' name.

We think this explains Troy's high-school experience. After putting his faith in Jesus as a high-school sophomore, he began to work on influencing his friends during his junior year. He seemed to consider each activity he was involved in and each circle of acquaintances as a chance to reach out. By the time he was a senior, he saw his school routine as a series of strategic evangelism sites. The two-hour chemistry lab at the end of each day afforded him great opportunity to talk about the Lord above the hum of the centrifuge. He hung out with the before-school bench jockeys so he could get a hearing for the gospel. As swim-team manager he served his team with enough good nature and excellence that he won their respect. His daily job in the student sales booth became a touch point for conversations with kids who were ready to talk about spiritual issues. He'd regularly invite people to church, Campus Life, and Young Life, often packing out his little car while giving rides. By the end of the first semester of his senior year, eighteen of his friends had put their faith in Jesus.

If you spend much time hunting for Troy-types (as we have), you'll find his story is more exceptional than normal. Certainly the Lord's timing, gifts, and calling are essential to understanding his case. But we think Troy also stumbled into the kind of strategic pattern for evangelism our Lord intended to be more common for Christians; it's most certainly effective among high-school students, where the social economy is anything but formal.

Didn't Jesus' leadership instruction teach us that to be faithful to our servant-leadership calling we can't clutch too much institutional power? He clearly dismissed James and John's bid for special seats of status as irrelevant to his purposes (Matthew 20:20-28). Jesus' leadership-development approach carried a paradigm-busting challenge with it. He asked his team to consider as their leadership standard not their lifelong encounters with ruler-types, but their present adventure with him. To make sure he was getting his point across, he washed their feet and invited them to join him at the end of the line, where the wait affords the greatest position for life-changing impact.

Jesus' anti-establishment vision of leadership fits nicely with the nature of social influence in today's youth culture. It only makes sense that we should bend our definition of student leadership to this biblical vision.

Defining Student Leadership in Youth Ministry

In the opening paragraph of this chapter you were introduced to Joel, Melissa, Sheri, Kenny, and Pat. Joel's efforts at influence almost naturally led to a more *formal* curriculum workbook. Melissa saw her gifts maximized when she was given the *formal* task of leading worship. That's similar to what happened with Kenny. Sheri saw the need for youth ministry and chose to create a *formal* organizational structure to meet the need. Pat's role in leadership began with a *formal* seat on the board pre-designated for a teenager. It was Pat's good fortune to be chosen.

All these student leaders shared at least one thing in common: They were highly visible. The *formal* structures and settings ensured a platform of recognition. Much of the secular research that has been done on leadership among adolescents locks onto this easy-to-see version of student leaders. They often approach their research by asking,

"Where are the students who lead?" This question begs for the formal-visible arenas to identify their chiefs. It's probably not too difficult even now to take a few minutes to see if you can identify the *formal* leaders in your local high school.

• Who are the publication editors?
• Who serves as president of each class?
• Who leads student government?
• What are the key clubs in the school, and who are the kids who lead them?
• Who captains each sports team?

While it shouldn't be too tough to discover these facts, not everyone thinks this represents the best way to understand leadership forces at work in a high-school community. There are a few research studies that take another approach. They begin to look at pockets of teenagers and ask, "Who leads these folks, and how?" Because this approach avoids starting with *formal* organizational structures, it tends to identify students who influence; they may or may not be visible outside their own influence group. Do you know who has emerged as the leader of that small band of students who gather to smoke on the corner each day? Who wields the most impact among those students who cluster in that out-of-the-way hall before the first bell rings every day? If the team captains are picked by coaches, it's fair to ask who *really* leads the members of a particular athletic squad. Multitudes of such influence pockets exist in every school community; how do these natural leaders operate?

The connection between visibility and leadership may seem obvious, at least on the surface. Those who are known by the most people have the opportunity to lead the greatest number of people. Highly visible formal platforms such as those identified above make it easy to identify some leaders. But as we noted above, this visibility is not essential to a definition of student leadership that seeks maximum, life-changing influence. As a matter of fact, significant research points to the greater influence exercised by close friends as contrasted with the influence of peers in general (Julia A. Graber, et al., eds, *Transitions Through Adolescence: Interpersonal Domains and Context*). Further, Jesus' teachings suggest that such spotlight visibility may not be necessary to accomplish his purposes.

We'd like to maintain that Joel, Melissa, Sheri, Kenny, and Pat should *not* be lifted up as standards of student leadership in youth ministry. It's not that they may not *be* student leaders; they just epitomize a false goal for student leadership. As important a role as they play in the kingdom, and as obviously invested in leadership as they are, our vision for student leadership must exceed that which can be accommodated by formal platforms and highly visible tasks. We shouldn't be asking how we can design our youth ministries so we can produce more Joels, Melissas, Sheris, Kennys, and Pats.

Student leaders in youth ministry are young people who demonstrate consistently that they take initiative and responsibility to reach their non-Christian peers for Christ and help them grow in Christ.

We should be asking how we can produce more Troys.

We want to define a vision of youth-ministry student leaders that is clear but flexible; it needs to provide direction without being unnecessarily prescriptive. From our discussion so far, it should be no surprise that we think peer influence is at the heart and soul of such a vision. See if the following definition rises to the standards described so far: Student leaders in youth ministry are young people who demonstrate consistently that they take initiative and responsibility to reach their non-Christian peers for Christ and help them grow in Christ.

Hopefully this definition of student leadership does more than align itself with the leadership-as-influence model we've discussed. It also specifies that Christian student leaders engage in evangelism, assume the burden of peer influence, and demonstrate behaviors that can be easily checked against standards of consistency.

Student Leaders' Goal: Peer Evangelism

Christians who are serious about world evangelism are familiar with three typically unrelated facts. First, teenagers represent one of the largest single demographic segments of the world's population. According to the United Nations' Population Division, well over one third of all people in the world are teenagers or younger. While trends indicate that this percentage will likely decline as the average life span lengthens in less-developed countries, the sheer mass of young people is growing at a staggering rate. To illustrate this fact, consider this: From 1804, when the world passed the 1 billion mark, it took 123 years to reach 2 billion people in 1927. It took another 33 years to attain 3 billion in 1960, 14 more years to reach 4 billion in 1974, and 13 more years to attain 5 billion in 1987. The world population was expected to reach the 6 billion mark in 1999, growing by a billion in just 12 years. This means more than 2 billion people in the world today are under twenty-six years of age, a number that—when taken by itself—is seven times the entire world's population in Jesus' day! (Taken from the United Nations Population Division, "1998 Revision of the World Population Estimates and Projections" World Wide Web site.)

Second, principles of peer-to-peer evangelism among teenagers are supported by established missionary findings identifying and categorizing the type of evangelism that is most effective. "E-1" evangelism is that which crosses a single frontier barrier, such as the gulf between those who are part of the church and those who aren't. "E-2" evangelism is characterized by those efforts that must cross a second frontier, one made up of significant but not huge differences in language and culture. Finally, "E-3" evangelism necessitates that a person crosses an even greater gulf in an effort to reach people who by language and culture are totally different. Ralph Winter observed that "E-1 evangelism—where a person communicates to his own people—is obviously the most potent kind of evangelism. People need to hear the gospel in their own language" (J.D. Douglas, ed., *Let the Earth Hear His Voice*).

Is there any doubt that teenager-to-teenager evangelism has greater effectiveness potential than most adult-to-teenager efforts (which, arguably, might be best labeled as E-2!)?

Third, many veterans in ministry would agree that the teenage years are when a significant number of conversions to Christianity take place. (There are real difficulties in designing research to verify this thesis. For example, if you choose to survey only those who are Christians currently—what else could you do—it would be difficult to factor in "deathbed conversions" and the like. Nonetheless, there seems to be a common consensus that some of our most important faith decisions take place during adolescence.)

One of the reasons suggested for this phenomenon is that there are heightened developmental factors contributing to a state of conversion readiness during adolescence. It also may be argued that this age group receives the most concentrated evangelism efforts. Regardless of reasons, and slippery though it has been to confirm this claim through empirical research, there aren't many that argue with it. More people make key choices to follow Christ during their teenage years than at any other time period in life.

When we pull these facts together for strategic ministry reflection, the implications become pretty clear. One of the primary reasons for the existence of specialized ministries to youth in the church must be to take advantage of this evangelism "window of opportunity" made possible at the intersection of demographic growth patterns and adolescent conversion readiness. Youth evangelism must be a priority of youth ministry. By extension, the most fruitful youth evangelism will be derived from strategies that have young people telling their friends the good news of life in Jesus Christ.

This is the strategy we wish to name "student leadership."

Are we implying that the only legitimate purposes for youth ministries circle around evangelism? No. Neither are we implying that the students who are leaders (call them whatever you will) must see peer evangelism as their only priority. We simply wish to make the case that in the grand smorgasbord of ministry done in Jesus' name, the main reason for creating a separate "youth buffet table" is evangelism. Further, the central entrée for a healthy diet on that table ought to be the practice of student leadership as we've defined it. (If you're hungry after these last two sentences, it's understandable!)

Student Leaders' Activity: Take Initiative and Responsibility

Adults all over the world invest themselves in youth ministry. Many of these often underpaid and overworked people would tell you that their greatest thrill is when a young person puts his or her faith in Jesus Christ. There is a joy-ride bonus for youth workers who have the privilege of praying with a teenager as he or she moves from spiritual death to life in Christ.

We'd better not let this greatest-of-celebration feeling mess with clear-minded ministry thinking. Let's check out an illustration.

Lots of mothers and fathers would be overjoyed to hear their children say they want to spend time at home. Unfortunately, as most kids grow older they seem less interested in hanging out with Mom and Dad. But think about it. If children only wanted to stay around home, would that not be cause for some concern in relation to their social development? Parents would recognize that it isn't in their children's best interest to always be homebound. Because they want their kids to grow into maturity and lean into life in healthy ways, they may choose parental ploys that kick them out of the nest.

Can we draw a parallel conclusion about spiritual maturity among young people? Don't we stunt the growth of our Christian teenagers if we encourage them to cultivate friendships exclusively with one another? Rather, we should recognize that teenage spiritual maturity is demonstrated by the hunger to copy our Lord as he related to everyone, including those who didn't believe in him. One application we can draw from Ephesians 4 is that we must be about equipping God's teenager-people for works of service until all of us are built up to maturity.

Some might wonder if teenagers can be so equipped. Can they "own" the responsibility of reaching their friends for Christ and helping them to grow in Christ? The description of our research findings throughout this book ought to help answer cautious folks on this matter. And even though there is ample evidence to affirm that the answers to these two questions are a resounding "yes," some youth workers—like some parents—will have a tough time letting go of their favorite ministry thrill (evangelism). Some of us meet our own needs to have our egos stroked by teenagers whose dependence on us feeds our own sense of worth. Whatever the motive, by our shortsightedness we fail to express true love to our teenagers, stunting their spiritual growth and inhibiting their contributions to the important work of God's kingdom.

Will all teenagers be able to grow until they take initiative and responsibility for reaching their peers? Probably not. But it doesn't follow logically that we're then somehow "exempt" from some of the Lord's expectations for every one of us. Jesus calls all members of his body to do their part. We aren't at liberty to "lower the bar" simply because our own experience suggests it might be rare for teenagers to step up to this serious task. In fact, we believe such nearsighted vision may contribute to unnecessary limitations being put on our teenagers. The sage who said, "The person who says 'I can' and the one who says 'I can't' are both right" has tapped into an insight about helping people rise to uncharted territories of personal accomplishment. We believe the Bible supplies both a vision and a challenge for student leaders to live up to. Our research has helped us confirm that youth ministries can actually pull off this faith-informed picture of what teenagers can accomplish when they're properly equipped to serve the Lord.

This book is being written because we, through Huntington College's Link Institute, were able to do a two-year study of student leadership in youth ministry. As you'll learn in the following chapters, there are plenty of students who take initiative and responsibility to reach their friends for Christ and help them grow in Christ. Just as significantly, there are a number of local youth ministries all over the country that have historically demonstrated an ability to mobilize students for a ministry of outreach to their peers. The following elaboration on our earlier definition of student leadership highlights the ownership that student leaders take in their peer ministry: Student leaders in youth ministry are young people who demonstrate consistently that they take initiative and responsibility to reach their non-Christian peers for Christ and help them grow in Christ. These students tend to view Christian adults and the programs they offer as available, but optional, resources for their ministry of peer outreach.

> Student leaders in youth ministry are young people who demonstrate consistently that they take initiative and responsibility to reach their non-Christian peers for Christ and help them grow in Christ. These students tend to view Christian adults and the programs they offer as available, but optional, resources for their ministry of peer outreach.

Can you imagine working with such motivated teenagers? What's more, can you imagine leading a youth ministry that regularly produces such student leaders? Before we offer helpful research-based insights on developing such student leaders, we need to complete our picture of the impressive qualities they possess.

Student Leaders' Reputation: Consistent Demonstration

Immature people are typically unpredictable and inconsistent. By contrast, mature folks possess an unflappable character quality that suggests a steady, consistent, and positive life—one able to withstand the closest scrutiny.

Most of us would agree that teenagers are typically in the "test-drive" stage of their maturity level. Judgments are often erratic, decision-making is impulsive, and raging hor-mones wield too much influence. Teenagers usually don't possess the depth of life expe-rience that is so valuable to critical thinking and focused direction.

Yet in the midst of the gaggle of teenagers bumping into each other at your local high school are a few that seem to be different. They are nearly *steady* in they way they live their lives! These exceptions to the norm whisper to us of the possibility of a life of consistent faithfulness to Jesus Christ, demonstrated daily by students who know that their hope for influence among their friends is wedded to the integrity of their lives.

And so we raise the bar of expectation. We insist that student leaders take seriously the standard of consistency because we know their spiritually starved peers will scrutinize their lives.

Student leaders meet the challenge.

The Need for a Clear Vision of Student Leadership

Without narrowly defining how student leaders should act, the picture we've tried to paint so far is one of teenagers who want so badly to reach their friends for Christ that they seek to build lives of consistent, Christlike behavior while they initiate efforts of in-fluence. We believe it's a strategic necessity to have a clear vision of what healthy student leaders look like. The goal needs to be clear if it will be useful in guiding us while we ac-tually try to *develop* such student leaders.

Some may want to hurry on to the task of developing their student leaders without possessing such a clear picture. They may not realize the harm that can come from their impatience. Foggy vision leads ministers to stumble blindly through their practices, wast-ing energy and remaining confused about the relationship between student leadership ef-forts (among others) and the really big life purposes God has designed for each of us. In other words, rather than participating in the grand tapestry our Lord is painting, our ef-forts might end up producing an unrelated artistic work of our own design. People with this foggy vision problem never really try to understand how everything they do in min-istry is supposed to fit together. They don't want to do the hard thinking when there is so much *activity* required. In fact, they are often excellent in doing youth ministry tasks well, they just haven't figured out how their particular performance could be adjusted to contribute to this vision of developing student leaders and further, how student leader-ship fits with the ultimate tasks our Lord assigns to us all.

Specialized ministry efforts, such as developing student leaders, ought to be driven by a clear vision. Somehow that particular vision must connect to the greatest and grandest vision our Lord has for us all. This connection helps to ensure that our efforts, in the final evaluation, receive a "well done!" from the Lord Jesus.

If the vision for student leadership is too narrow or disconnected from God's overall designs, we will be in danger of misdirection. This could lead to inflating the importance of student leadership at the expense of, say, the overall health of the church. For example, if student leaders such as Melissa (at the beginning of the chapter) are asked to invest themselves in worship practice and training, it's hard to imagine that being a bad thing. But what if, because of the energy required by Melissa to be ready to lead worship at the level of quality expected, she has no time to build bridges to the non-Christians in her world? Multiply that scenario throughout the world, and the end result may be a church that, in the future, has wonderfully popular and meaningful worship services but is clueless about how to effectively share faith in the culture.

Our definition of student leadership is intended to lodge this youth ministry strategy squarely in the camp of those who see the church's greatest task as fulfilling the Great Commission's mandate of making disciples.

Beyond Definition as Vision

We have intended to stake out a clear definition of student leadership in youth ministry, one that will serve as a guiding vision for specific efforts. This definition is rooted in our understanding of Scripture rather than a survey of popular ministry practices. We believe the grand river of God's ultimate purpose distributes itself into a number of different tributaries; when the stream of youth ministry is considered, a defined peer-evangelism strategy that we have chosen to call *student leadership* emerges.

This definition of student leadership was at the heart of Link Institute's National Student Leadership Research Project. The remainder of the book is devoted to sharing insights from this research about developing student leaders for youth evangelism. In the next chapter we'll share why a disciple-making focus is essential to producing student leaders. Chapter 3 explains the role adults need to play when student leadership is fully operational. Chapters 4 through 6 describe how the most effective student leaders seem to dance through the peer-influence party in their world while making a graceful impact. What emerges is a clean and crisp job description for student leaders, something we call the Student Leader Three-Step.

One surprising bonus of our research was when we stumbled onto some fascinating findings about how different stages of vitality for a youth ministry seem to be excellent predictors of evangelism effectiveness. That's the focus of the seventh chapter. In chapter 8 we do a quick survey of some standardized approaches to student leadership, scrutinizing common practices in light of our research. In our ninth chapter we consider the social development factors that may influence youth workers' practical decisions in student leadership. Finally, we offer our best planning tips for youth ministries who want to maximize the effectiveness of student leadership.

We are enthusiastic about the role student leaders can play in youth ministry. Far from being incidental to our dreams, student leaders may be the most significant people participating in the cause of youth evangelism. Where do we find them?

Or how do we grow them?

CHAPTER 2:
The Disciple-Making Focus of Student Leadership

Little league baseball coaches trying to introduce the fine art of hitting to their teams understand the complementary roles of vision and focus. To produce a vision—or feel—of what a good hit is like, the coach might use a batting tee or throw a bucket of balls to each player. Kids need to be able to picture the ball jumping off the bat as solid contact is made. They need to be sold on the preferable value of the frozen-rope line drive over the fly ball. In fact, the counterproductive vision of a home run sailing over the fence can lead to a swing that results in too many pop ups or strikeouts. When the vision is locked in, coaches find much greater fruitfulness as they talk about the elements of focus while hitting.

"Don't just see the ball when it comes in, see a spot on the ball."

"Hit the ball when it gets right in front of the plate."

"Watch the ball hit the bat, keeping your head down all the way."

Batters might get small Wiffle balls thrown to them so they can improve their focus as they swing. It's fair to say that once a truly compelling vision is in place, energies should be fully devoted to improving one's focus. Sharply focused hitters will be the most likely to attain their batting goal (vision).

In the previous chapter, we introduced the goal of student leadership. It's likely that this entire book will have a vision-clarifying agenda for many readers. In the end, it will be critical that we emerge with an ability to articulate a vision of student leadership. But hammering away at vision, constantly declaring it until it becomes familiar, is not sufficient to reach our goal in student leadership. We must know how to coach the process of development, understanding the details of growth and maturation that lead to student leadership.

We need the right focus—a disciple-making focus—to lead us to our student-leadership vision.

The Danger of an Errant Focus

An errant focus suggests that ministry energy is being either diffused or concentrated in the wrong areas. Folks with a focus problem struggle in the way they manage their efforts and time. At week's end they may feel legitimately drained from their activity but bewildered about the fruitfulness of their efforts. To borrow a concept popularized by Stephen Covey, urgent matters crowd out important ones (Stephen R. Covey, et al., *First Things First*). The things done may, in fact, be done very well. Perhaps that's why it's difficult for the focus-impaired to consider whether *what* they spend their time doing should even be done at all.

Vision and focus are two sides of the coin of effective ministry. People with clear vision and faulty focus seem to understand the ultimate direction their youth ministry ought to take. They just don't do a good job with the daily details and processes of ministry, which are the ultimate test of effectiveness. What is important is clear; what to do next in order to accomplish what is important is the mystery.

Focus-driven people are just the opposite. These folks are sharp in their ability to manage youth-ministry efforts, but they haven't come to see what the God-ordained end of their efforts ought to be. Dangerously passive, they don't know where their activity is leading. They may not have spent much time considering what is important, but they are clear about what to do next. Borrowing from Peter F. Drucker's distinctions in *The Effective Executive*, they major on efficiency (doing things right) rather than effectiveness (doing the right things).

We need a laser beam approach to our youth ministry, where we guide our efforts (focus) so they're locked onto the proper target (vision). Too often our energy is pointed in the wrong direction or so diffused that it casts a soft harmless light when young people need high-tech spiritual surgery. In the previous chapter, we advanced the case for establishing a clear vision of student leaders as those young people who take initiative to reach their friends for Christ and help them grow in Christ. If we are going to zero in on the kind of efforts needed to develop these student leaders, we need to beware of some competing tugs for our attention. See if any of the following are tempting focus points in your ministry.

The Center of Attention

A pastor recently described his work in terms that recall the employees who hustle around the local pizza buffet making sure that there are plenty of different pizzas and the salad bar is well-stocked. He sees ministry as *providing opportunities* for people to come to Christ, grow in Christ, or be helped to serve Christ. What individuals do with those opportunities is largely up to them. According to this approach, ministry effectiveness increases when the programs offered match the needs and wants of those who are being served. Offer the right pizza in the right amount at the right time, and the buffet will draw a crowd.

Chances are pretty good that people will get fed this way. Will everyone get what they want? Recent experiences suggest that it might take the aggressiveness of a hockey player to get our pizza of preference! If an employee were watching us when we fell short of getting those last pieces of taco pizza, he or she would not have had a hard time reading our frustration. But what if the employee were concentrating exclusively on the pizza quantities, making sure to stay ahead of the demand, assuming people will get the food they want? It seems the local pizza establishment would miss out on learning whether they're satisfying customers (like us!) with special cravings. We'll eventually go elsewhere.

This illustration parallels program-centered approaches to ministry. It also reflects a subtly errant ministry focus. Pizza-buffet-monitoring is no substitute for direct assessment of customer satisfaction. Such a business strategy would likely prove costly to a pizza place. In the same way, monitoring our ministry programs may lead us to conclude that we are effective, even though direct investigation of the spiritual progress of people could reveal otherwise. For example, a well-attended youth ministry is not the most accurate indicator that teenagers are growing in Christ. Our focus is off-center.

Let's push this pizza-selling analogy a bit further before taking our early lunch break. A pure ministry-buffet approach is customer-want driven. Consequently, we assume that if our programs are gobbled up by our people, we're doing good ministry. There may be danger in that assumption.

Here's the point. The moment we think of student leadership as a program, our focus will get fuzzy. It's not because we can't use programs to develop student leaders; in fact, we'll likely need to use some effective programs to reach our goals. But we dare not let our evaluative eyes wander away from the important object of focus: the student leaders themselves.

The key to escaping a program-centered approach to ministry is not in avoiding programs, but in assessing them for their effectiveness in helping teenagers grow in their

Christian maturity and faithfulness. Sonlife Ministries has done the body of Christ a great service by articulating, first for youth ministry and then for healthy churches, a biblical process of ministry that champions the Great Commission. Early on, they may have obscured their purpose with the suggestion that ministry health is best assessed by diagnosing program balance. (Actually, Sonlife's definition of programs goes a long way toward remedying this problem.) It does not necessarily follow that mature and faithful Christians (M7 is Sonlife's designation) will need the assistance of church-developed programs in order to share their faith with others. Our conviction is that we are less likely to misstep when we *focus* on developing people rather than programs.

There are other candidates that compete for the center-soul of our approach to youth ministry. Some ministries may be building-centered, with a sort of "field of dreams" philosophy. "If we build it (and maintain it and feature it...) they will come (and be ministered to)." When Howard A. Snyder warned churches to beware of an "edifice complex" in *Radical Renewal: The Problem of Wineskins Today*, he was addressing this potential error. It may be that student leaders can't conceive of their jobs apart from some physical property or location. How ironic! Student leadership—conceived precisely because it takes advantage of the natural "while going through life" mobility of teenagers—can become restrictive because "come to our place" ministry assumptions prevail.

Other ministries may be word-centered, led by people who are convinced that if the right things are said in the right way by the right people, good ministry takes place. More subtle than the earlier illustrations, this practice also represents a dangerous error in focus. Youth workers who are convinced that their obligation is fulfilled because they have delivered the right words might be tempted to evaluate the rightness of their words in the isolation of their study. But people can be faithful to the text without even being in touch with their audience. We never just teach the Bible; we teach *people* the Bible. Paul's self-described philosophy in 1 Corinthians 9 shows how person-centeredness impacts the gospel word-crafting that occupies so much of the ministry we need to have among young people.

Some ministries are even bottom-line (money) centered. The focus of attention regularly goes to a financial balance sheet, and when the numbers look good, there is a sense of relief—the ministry must be healthy. Parachurch youth organizations that pack their boards with businesspeople who are better at raising money than raising questions about ministry direction ought not to be surprised at the agenda when the gavel falls. Student leadership is usually at the investment end—rather than the revenue end—of our ministry efforts.

What's the point of all this navel-gazing? Just this: Ministry must always be centered—that is, conceptually anchored—around the vision of developing people toward Christ-likeness. In biblical terms, this is making disciples. We in youth ministry must understand that disciple-making begins with evangelism and progresses as students grow in maturity and faithfulness. *Student leadership must be located in this process.*

Why maturity and faithfulness? These two terms, when taken together, are sufficient to describe the profile of any disciple, including student leaders. In fact, the difference between student leaders and other students involved in youth ministry is largely a difference in *degree of maturity* and *consistency of faithfulness.*

The reality is that maturity and faithfulness combine just the right blend of person-centered flexibility with objective standards. It's possible to take any young person's pulse of progress at any particular time along the parallel roads of maturity and faithfulness. Of course, we need to be focused directly on our young people to assess such progress. Then we'll get a good handle on who is ready for student leadership.

Before taking a closer look at these important focus points for our disciple-making efforts, let's examine a model for understanding how all of us—including student leaders—are put together. Wouldn't it be great if we newly focused, person-centered youth workers were also clear in understanding what God's master design is for every young person we work with? As a bonus it might affect not just what we try to accomplish in the lives of those we minister *to,* but how we see our obligation to those we minister *with.* Student leaders fall into both categories.

What are the consequences when youth ministry is done by those who don't see the big picture for people? Well…

Rich is leaving his current ministry. He's been effective in the task he was asked to do, but a few months ago the frustration and anger were beginning to gain leverage in his life. Underpaid, underappreciated, and overburdened…this young man desperately needed someone to help him see his life in larger perspective. Instead, he stumbled on, rolling up seventy to eighty hours a week in a cause that had invigorated him at one time.

Consider the case of Jill, a popular high-school student especially valued for her ability to attract other kids to youth meetings. As a student leader she is hugely appreciated by her zealous

Why maturity and faithfulness? These two terms, when taken together, are sufficient to describe the profile of any disciple, including student leaders. In fact, the difference between student leaders and other students involved in youth ministry is largely a difference in *degree of maturity* and *consistency of faithfulness.*

youth director, but he doesn't know that she desperately wishes she could find the courage to talk with someone about her sexual identity struggles.

Meet Fred, a talented all-scholastic, all-star student who can do so much for his youth ministry that they ask a great deal...without regard for how the long hours and scattered focus impact Fred's ability to be a faithful family member, friend, student, or athlete.

The local youth church is never so attractive as when Julie is involved. She throws herself into every meeting with contagious enthusiasm, drawing praise from her youth pastor for her contributions to the kingdom. The only problem is that when Julie relates to her non-Christian classmates in the routines of her high-school experience, she acts differently and communicates a picture of God's kingdom that is both unattractive and inaccurate.

There's a lot at stake here. In our performance-oriented culture, when kingdom tasks are divvied up throughout the body, there is a better-than-average chance that the big picture might get lost in the shuffle. Whose responsibility is it to protect our own wholeness and spiritual health? How can it be OK for us to ask more and more of our student leaders without regard for the potential of contributing to the fragmentation of their lives?

We sometimes act as if involving harried kids in the work of particular ministries will bring about God-honoring fruit just because the work is important. We act as if our youth ministry specialization absolves us from reckoning with a person's all-of-life responsibilities before God. Two notorious examples from our contemporary culture ought to remind us of the consequences of such neglect. O.J. Simpson attained his celebrity icon status not by virtue of his entire life, but because of limited, specialized accomplishments on the football field (and to a lesser degree, in movies). President Bill Clinton insisted that his job performance was all that mattered, and the American people largely agreed. Our culture doesn't seem to have the mechanisms to express concern for whole-person development. It's troubling that our ministry culture is so similar.

We need to break this cycle in our disciple-making focus with student leaders. If we are to be person-centered in our ministry with—and to—student leaders, we must have a wholistic understanding of people. We must have a clear picture of what God's creative purposes for us are and how the unique and common features of our humanness have been built into the fabric of our lives. *And we must be convinced that our disciple-making energies will result in more, not less, ministry effectiveness because they honor rather than ignore God's master plan for people.*

In the Beginning...

It's clear that the very core of life is derived from our God-given spirit. We are essentially spiritual beings. When there was only a dusty shell, Adam was almost, but not quite born. Life began from the very breath of God (Genesis 2:7). And when sin entered the world, all humankind was cut off from the very life that was our essence...that is, until Jesus entered the world. He took on our sin so that through him and in him we might receive the life of God once again (2 Corinthians 5:21; Colossians 3:3-4). We are essentially spiritual people, created for a life-union with God, and we're privileged to reconnect with our essence through faith in Jesus Christ (Galatians 2:20). It is this wonderful mystery that Lawrence Richards is referring to when he describes the task of ministry as that of nurturing "faith-as-life" (Lawrence O. Richards, *Christian Education: Seeking to Become Like Jesus Christ*).

The Genesis account also identifies three additional human capacities for which we were all created. Consider the following passage:

"The Lord God took the man and put him in the Garden of Eden to work it and take care of it. And the Lord God commanded the man, 'You are free to eat from any tree in the garden; but you must not eat from the tree of the knowledge of good and evil, for when you eat of it you will surely die.' The Lord God said, 'It is not good for the man to be alone. I will make a helper suitable for him' " (Genesis 2:15-18).

First of all, notice that the creation account identifies us as essentially *responsible* people. God assigned a garden-minding task to Adam at a particular location, testifying to the nature of his newly created masterpiece by his act of delegation. We were made to do things, to accomplish good works laid out for us by the Lord Jesus (Ephesians 2:10). The Lord God placed specific expectations upon Israel for observing feast days (Leviticus 23), constructing the Tabernacle (Exodus 35–40), and conquering Jericho (Joshua 6). Jesus assigned jobs of various importance to his disciples, from Passover preparation (Mark 14:13-16) to itinerant preaching (Luke 10:1-21). Paul understood his God-given tasks in both sweeping (Acts 20:24) and specific ways (1 Corinthians 9). There is perhaps no more dramatic illustration of the truth that we were created to be responsible agents than the astounding formal entrustment of the disciple-making task to the disciples and, by extension, to all of us who follow Christ (Matthew 28:19-20). Before God we are responsible to do what Jesus wants us to do. Anything more is superfluous, anything less insufficient. God will not ask us to do anything we cannot do (Philippians 2:13), and since we were created as responsible agents, faithfulness is the expectation God lays on us.

Second, notice that even before sin had entered the world, there was an expectation that man could make *moral* distinctions. God drew boundaries; right and wrong was a simple matter of obedience to him. The Bible offers plenty of examples of this uncomplicated moral base. Big brother Cain offered God a sacrifice from the fruit of his own labors which was unacceptable; it did not meet God's specifications (Abel got it right) (Genesis 4). Abraham prepared to plunge a knife into his long-awaited son upon learning that this was the action God (apparently!) required of him (Genesis 22:1-18). Moses' seemingly innocuous action of striking rather than simply speaking to the rock eliminated him from entering into the Promised Land with the rest of Israel (Numbers 20). Saul lost the blessing of God when he thought Samuel's tardiness sufficient reason to become designated-sacrificer (1 Samuel 13:1-14). We have been created with a moral capacity, and the expectation is that in doing what God has instructed us to do, we will display the same obedient character as that of Jesus Christ—resulting in similar fruitfulness (John 15:1-12; Galatians 5:22-25; Hebrews 5:8).

There is an interesting body of social science research that indicates that from an early age we make distinctions between matters of morality and simple social convention when faced with decisions of right or wrong. Children from all different backgrounds are able to understand that, for example, while it may be wrong to chew gum in Mrs. Snider's class because of her rules, it would be OK if there were no prohibitions against chomping away. Yet, rules or no rules, it is always wrong to hit another child (Elliot Turiel, *The Development of Social Knowledge: Morality and Convention*). If we are not created with a moral capacity, where does such an inner compass come from?

Finally, we have been created as *relational* beings. God's observation was that there is something wrong with man when he is alone, isolated, and without a partner. This is not to put down the special ministry-enhancing gift of celibacy (1 Corinthians 7), but to affirm that we have been designed as social animals. As we grow, we move out of relational dependence to independence...and then on to interdependence. In one of the most common expressions of who we are, Scripture identifies Christians as the body of Jesus Christ, to be corporately responsive to his direction as head (1 Corinthians 12; Colossians 1:15-21). In order to help us pull off this harmonic functioning, a lot of Scripture is intended to help us experience the quality of relationships for which our Lord created us. We learn that the abuse of power is never an option (Matthew 20:25-28), that class favoritism is wrong (James 2:1-7), and that our personal sin is a corporate concern (1 Corinthians 5; Galatians

6:1-2). We are to be patient with one another (Ephesians 4:2), forgive one another (Colossians 3:13), and take an active role in helping each other be faithful (Hebrews 10:24).

As these illustrations suggest, the way our Lord asks us to relate to others is often in direct contrast with the mantra of our popular culture where, for example, an individual's right to privacy and the pursuit of self-interest are considered sacred. The standard of expectation for our relationships is as demanding as it is straightforward: relate to people as Jesus Christ wants us to, drawing on his example and his Spirit for both guidance and strength.

Here are the common grand purposes for which we were all created. This is as true for student leaders as it is for those of us who want to recruit and develop student leaders. At their innermost core they must access their very life from God through faith in Jesus Christ. Drawing on the spirit-quickening presence of Jesus at the center of their lives, they are to become Christlike in character (moral), treat other people as Christ would (relational/social), and do in word and deed only those things that can be done in the name of Jesus Christ (responsible/vocational). When we focus on student leaders as unique people, with disciple-making in mind, we dare not ignore this creative template by which we all were made.

Habermas and Issler provide a clear articulation of these four functional ends of mankind (they label them communion, character, community, and commission). In rounding out an understanding of the created nature of people, they also call attention to the common structural elements—personality, intelligence, physical attributes—which are part of the unique package God has given to each of us (Ronald Habermas and Klaus Issler, *Teaching for Reconciliation: Foundations and Practice of Christian Educational Ministry*). Our adaptation of their work, where the Lord's gifts are included as part of the outer endowment circle, is graphically represented below:

Student Leader Maturity As a Disciple-Making Focus

It is critical to understand how the three areas of character formation (moral), relational orientation (social), and task obligations (vocational) are dependent upon our spiritual core, where faith is developed as it helps us experience the life-gift of Jesus Christ. Insightful questions can help unlock the nature of this connection as we work to disciple student leaders. Consider the following three:

• As it reflects character formation, "Are you *becoming who* the Lord Jesus wants you to become?"

• As it reflects relational orientation, "Are you *relating to others* as the Lord Jesus wants you to relate?"

• As it reflects task obligations, "Are you *doing what* the Lord Jesus wants you to do?"

In order for any of us to pursue satisfactory answers to these questions, we need to know the Lord Jesus and what he wants. The essence of faith development is to grow in the knowledge of Jesus Christ. The key question to assess student leaders' faith-as-life core is, "How truly and personally do you know Jesus Christ?"

> In order for any of us to pursue satisfactory answers to these questions, we need to know the Lord Jesus and what he wants. The essence of faith development is to grow in the knowledge of Jesus Christ. The key question to assess student leaders' faith-as-life core is, "How truly and personally do you know Jesus Christ?"

Because Jesus really exists, we can be either accurate or off-base in our knowledge of him. We need to know him *truly.*

Because Jesus really cares, we can build a relationship with him as we walk through our life with him. We need to know him *personally.*

Some in our culture invite us to consider *only* the Jesus of our own experience, claiming that our personal encounter is all the truth we need. At the other extreme are those who can clinically dissect the truth about Jesus but cannot identify a reservoir of life-changing experiences that testify to the reality that Jesus Christ has been active in their personal transformation. Both of these approaches are inadequate.

Clearly, helping student leaders nurture the faith at the very core of their existence is critical to their ability to fulfill the ends for which they were created, and their faith growth is dependent upon their personal knowledge of Jesus Christ. We cannot hope to help student leaders take on Christlike character, relate to others like Jesus, or be faithful in accomplishing what he wants if their understanding of him is inaccurate...or so abstract that it's disconnected from the complicated realities of their own lives. If student leaders are valued only because they *do* evangelism, they likely won't be nurtured in a growing relationship with Jesus Christ.

The biblical term to describe the desired goal of such faith is *maturity*. In the parable of the sower (Luke 8:4-15), the seed that is choked out by thorns—life's worries, riches, and pleasures—doesn't have a chance to reach the *maturity* for which it was intended. Paul could speak a message of wisdom among those who were *mature* (1 Corinthians 2). He felt that those who were *mature* would be able to understand that the clear priority of knowing and gaining Christ would, by comparison, make any other pursuit like wallowing in a rubbish pile (Philippians 3). The apostle also gave *maturity* an end-point status in his description of the pattern of ministry (Ephesians 4). He further identified *maturity* as the goal of Epaphras' prayer for the Colossians, that they "may stand firm in all the will of God, mature and fully assured" (Colossians 4:12b). The writer of Hebrews used the word "maturity" as a practical benchmark to distinguish people who may still be learning the elementary teachings about Christ (Hebrews 6:1) from those who are ready for a more solid spiritual diet. Those who are *mature* attained such status as a result of continuously practicing their understanding of the rule of Jesus in their lives (Hebrews 5:14). James links maturity to our ability to hang in there as learners until the toughest teacher of all—life's difficult experiences—can bring about our character transformation (James 1:2-4).

The picture of maturity in Scripture sketches people who are so deeply rooted in biblical truth that Jesus Christ operates as the unchallenged Lord of their lives. *We will have confidence that our student leaders' faith is mature when it helps them know Jesus Christ both truly and personally, and he is established as the central filter in their lives.* They will learn biblical truth in two ways: (1) as they are instructed in its content, and (2) as they experience its reality. Each of these is essential to their maturation.

	Biblical truth as reality learned by experience	Biblical truth as reality *not* yet learned by experience
Biblical truth as content learned by instruction	Mature	Less mature
Biblical truth as content *not* yet learned by instruction	Less mature	Immature

Let's consider for a moment that we want to equip our student leaders to do peer evangelism. We may sign them up for some formal classes and require some significant reading. There are those who, because of their diligent studies, will learn the content required in this course very well. If there were tests they would excel, and if there were grades reflecting only their cognitive understanding of the material, they would be sitting pretty.

But while these goals might be adequate for an academic class, they're not sufficient for our student leaders. We want them to experience the sweaty-palm nervousness that comes right before engaging someone in a spiritual conversation for the first time. We want them to listen to their own excuses for their evangelism *inactivity* which are so reasonable and loud that the Holy Spirit's voice is tough to pick up. We want them to encounter the diversity of their friends, some who are hungry for the gospel and some apathetic to the gospel, and realize that they're equally needy. Somehow, if they're really going to learn to reach their friends, they must experience the related realities of evangelism.

The same is true for all of our Christian faith because Jesus Christ did not come to be a teacher of precepts, but to give us life. We ought to teach young people the great, sweeping content of scriptural truth. We ought to help them study the details of biblical instruction. But we also must coach them to learn the realities of God's Word in the daily routines of our lives. Both of these elements are included in an understanding of maturity.

What if a student is effectively reaching his or her friends but knows only the five verses contained in a favorite evangelism tract? We hope you'll agree that the need for biblical maturity in such a teenager's life is strong. We must never let short-term evangelism successes keep us from focusing on a long-term disciple-making focus. That focus also includes *faithfulness*.

Student Leader Faithfulness as a Disciple-Making Focus

Understanding maturity is crucial to understanding how faithfulness is a distinct concept, worthy of its own person-centered focus in our student-leadership efforts. Maturity seems to carry with it a sense of arrival or attainment. While it shouldn't be confused with the ultimate end of perfection, it is a critical benchmark in our becoming like Jesus.

Faithfulness, on the other hand, relates exclusively to our *obedience* to God. Each opportunity of life presents a new opportunity to be faithful. As such, the context of any specific situation, including a person's gifts, abilities, experiences, insights, and God's personal directives are critical to understanding whether or not someone was faithful. The Bible indicates that faithfulness in smaller matters is a prerequisite for greater opportunities (Luke 19:11-26). Patterns of faithfulness are likely more up and down than those of maturity. Student leaders—or young people in general—certainly are at no faithfulness disadvantage due to their age.

How do we get a handle on faithfulness? If our youth ministry vision and focus are to be connected to this ideal, how can we assess our effectiveness? It may be helpful to consider how evaluating a student leader's faithfulness would differ from assessing his or her maturity.

We know maturity is assessed in the same way children are determined to be able to go on the wilder rides at an amusement park. "You must be this tall," the sign says. Once someone reaches the required height, he or she is tall enough to grab the thrill. Similarly, once a young person has developed a sufficient level of understanding about God and God's expectations, that person may be said to be mature.

By contrast, faithfulness is constantly open to measurement, married as it is to the moments of life. For example, a student leader who has had an impeccable record of faithfulness over a two-year period may, in a weak moment, find that she or he has "missed the mark" and stands in need of repentance. As such, faithfulness probably is best assessed by considering one's consistency of living. This is not unlike how a basketball player judges free throw effectiveness (the percentage of baskets made in relation to the opportunities to go to the line describes one's consistency).

If we want to help student leaders' (or anyone's!) character development, relationships, and responsibilities, we must focus on increasing their faithfulness. As moral people, we want to be no more or less than the people Jesus wants us to be. As social beings, we want to relate to others exactly as Jesus would want us to relate to them. Finally, as people created for responsibility, we want to be so in tune with the Lord that we can discern exactly what service he requires of us, and then have the courage to do just exactly what he wants. Every opportunity of life presents itself as a chance to be faithful again to the Lord...or not. Like the basketball player, our *progress* will be evident as we become more consistent. To further illustrate, someone who regularly makes just five out of ten attempts would love to increase the percentage of shots converted. If we respond faithfully in only five out of every ten life-chances, our clear goal becomes increasing our consistency in faithfulness. We can celebrate six out of ten while setting our eyes on perfection. Presumably this is what it means to be "more faithful."

Faithfulness is identified by Jesus as one of the more important matters of the law...which was hypocritically neglected by some religious leaders (Matthew 23:23). Parables point to the responsibility of those who are faithful, and that faithfully fulfilling the assigned responsibility will earn a person opportunities for even greater responsibilities

(Matthew 24:45; 25:21-23). Many of the references to faithfulness in the New Testament are descriptions of particular people. Thus the term is defined in the examples of Timothy (1 Corinthians 4:17), the Ephesians (Ephesians 1:1), Epaphras (Colossians 1:7), Onesimus (Colossians 4:9), the Colossians (Colossians 1:2), Tychicus (Ephesians 6:21; Colossians 4:7), Moses (Hebrews 3:2, 5), Silas (1 Peter 5:12), and Gaius (3 John 3, 5). Faithfulness is an important descriptor used by John in his futuristic vision of the saints of God (Revelation 2:10, 13; 13:10; 14:12; 17:14), besides being the name of the Lord Jesus as the white horse rider (Revelation 19:11).

We are admonished by Paul to be faithful in prayer (Romans 12:12), prove our faithfulness after we have been given a trust (1 Corinthians 4:2), and walk in the Spirit in such a way that faithfulness is an evident fruit (Galatians 5:21, 22-23). Paul's amazement at being chosen by God for service may be surpassed only by his thankfulness for being considered faithful (1 Timothy 1:12).

No doubt Paul's jaw-dropping awe is due in part to his appreciation of the perfect faithfulness of the Lord Jesus in relation to us (1 Thessalonians 5:24; 2 Timothy 2:13; Hebrews 2:17). This is a great example of how maturity and faithfulness relate to each other. Our understanding of the Lord Jesus actually filters anything we hear from him. When we know him to be perfectly faithful to accomplish in us that which he calls us to do, when we're certain that his call to us comes from his great love for us and others, our own resolve to be faithful is strengthened. We experience not only a clear sense of direction from the Lord regarding our character, relationships, and tasks, but also the active empowering efforts of the Holy Spirit related to our motivation and perseverance.

Can you see why mere programs of student leadership will be insufficient to meet this depth of need? Person-centeredness—with its disciple-making focus—gives us a chance.

It is our contention that if we're clear about our grand purposes while we go about our youth ministry tasks, we can help students grow in maturity and faithfulness. Whatever else we do, we must focus on facilitating this growth. As the following matrix shows, it is strategically useful to be able to understand where young people are in their own maturity and faithfulness. Student leaders can be readily identified by virtue of their maturity and faithfulness in relation to their peers. Not insignificantly, these are the very qualities that will provide them with the authority to influence their friends. Finally, we'll be able to pinpoint with person-centered accuracy the most urgent needs our student leaders have as they progress toward Christlikeness.

	Mature	Immature
Consistently faithful	Needed: encouragement to persevere	Needed: instruction and/or experience in the truth
Inconsistently faithful	Needed: reminders and support	Needed: support and growth in truth
Consistently unfaithful	Needed: loving challenge to repent	Needed: confrontation with the truth incarnate (Christ)

A Final Challenge

We are about to move into a consideration of specific things adults can do to help ensure that student leaders grow in maturity and faithfulness. Before leaving a chapter where we presented a model for each person's all-of-life development, it may be worthwhile to consider what we, as youth workers, bring to this task of student-leader development. How is our maturity level? What patterns of faithfulness have been working in our own lives? Jesus' words have powerful implications for the life-transfusion process he calls us to in disciple-making: "A student is not above his teacher, but everyone who is fully trained will be like his teacher" (Luke 6:40).

Some may think this chapter has diverged from the focus of student leadership. "At the very least," an eager youth worker might protest, "there's not much that's practical here." Nothing could be further from the truth. Student leadership begins after we decide *who* will be a part of our team. Use this understanding of maturity and faithfulness to establish your criteria for selecting student leaders. Ask what sort of vision for their task can be expected from student leaders who are mature but not faithful. How will this vision differ from that of students who are faithful but immature believers? The prospect of a student leader's vision for ministry emerging from a life that is other than mature and faithful should be a forceful reminder of the pre-eminence of these two qualities in people-development.

We can see the importance of considering how maturity and faithfulness impact one's ministry vision and focus. The stakes are high for our student leaders.

For adults, too.

CHAPTER 3:
The Role of Adults in Student Leadership

Mick believes student leaders are absolutely essential players in reaching teenagers for Christ. He also thinks his role is to "ride herd" on the most mature students to help them maximize ministry effectiveness. On the other hand, Emily believes that we adults have exercised unnecessary control in youth ministry. If students are going to grow as leaders, she is convinced they need to be exposed to, not protected from, the pressures, obligations, and frustrations of leadership. Emily sees herself as a resource for enterprising teenagers. Mick is a coach, developing talent. Who's right?

Wouldn't it be wonderful if, as a result of either our research findings or the clear teaching of Scripture, we could list the three things adults need to do in order to produce student leaders who are mature, faithful, and effective in evangelism?

It's not that simple.

But we have found a nice overlap between biblical disciple-making principles and what our research surfaced about the roles adults ought to play in student-leadership development. Maybe both Mick and Emily are right. We'll learn in this chapter that adults need to be on their toes as they relate to their student leaders. While it might be a real stretch to ask adults to be flexible, our conclusions are pretty clear. We need to be alert if we will provide the responsive, person-centered disciple-making that leads to effective student leadership. As you consider the following four disciple-making principles, be sure to note how our research spotlights at least one dimension of how the modern practice of student leadership—in its most effective form—captures timeless truth from God's Word.

Be Clear Enough to Be Intentional

This principle has been developed in some depth throughout the first two chapters. *Adults must have a clear vision of the outcome they are seeking through student leadership if they are to focus their energies productively.* Building from the previous chapter, our focus ought to be on making disciples of each individual in our sphere of influence, recognizing that student leaders *emerge* out of such a faithful process. When Dann Spader, Sonlife's founder, teaches his seminars, he often uses the imagery of popcorn kernels popping to describe how we might identify these emerging leaders.

Notice how different this process is from management-informed approaches to recruiting and screening students for leadership. Under that way of thinking, youth workers send out a wide invitation to teenagers, get responses on lengthy application forms, check references, and conduct probing interviews. Even when it's done thoroughly, that process can't possibly compete with what we learn about students while making disciples.

We hope these four principles of disciple-making might shed some light on the ways our Lord assembled his original "student leader" team. Let's start by taking a close look at the original mandate for making disciples.

The sole command in the Great Commission (Matthew 28:18-20) is to make disciples. "Go," "baptizing," and "teaching them to obey" are used to modify that command. We need to see disciple-making as a task not just for the specialists, but for us all. Somehow we adult youth leaders must focus not only on the task in our ministry to teenagers; we must also pass it on to them. They, too, are obligated to help make disciples.

Most translations of the Great Commission imply that we're commanded to go to other locations—like missionaries overseas—in order to make disciples. This might have been true if the participle "going" (perhaps more accurately understood as "while going") was used instead of the imperative "go." We don't mean to say it's not important to travel to faraway places to serve the Lord, if that's where we're called. But this passage simply doesn't teach that. Instead it affirms the obligation of disciple-making as a way of life for all of us.

One of the great joys for all ministers is when their disciples use opportunities in their natural life-arenas to make other disciples. "While going" is as natural as it gets. When Joel wanted to reach others for Christ, it only made sense for him to start a Bible study with other guys on the basketball team. We've got to help our student leaders develop deep, transformational contacts with others as part of the normal ebb and flow of their lives. Isn't it clear that they will have at least some advantages over adults when it comes to this avenue of teenager ministry? The youth culture is where a student leader's natural life journey takes place. We adults need to be deliberate and courageous when we cross bridges to hang out in the "land of the teenager." As we'll see later, there may be good reasons for adults to take such journeys.

"Baptizing" points to the incorporative goal of disciple-making, reminding us that when we help people become who God wants them to be, we must bring them into the family of believers united under Jesus' lordship. The small groups we observed in our research often facilitated depths of body-accountability in the lives of the best student leaders. Jason, Thad, Shea, and Jordan cite their weekly small-group Bible study with Nate as the most important ingredient in their Christian growth, largely because they have been able to be honest with one another. They experience a sense of gospel partnership through such a group. Doesn't it seem that Christian brothers and sisters who are most like us will best handle the accountability portion of our participation in the body of Christ? People "like us" are less easily dismissed when they remind us of our obligations to Christ. The boys identified above would agree that it's a good idea for student leaders to meet with their friends on a regular basis.

"Teaching them to obey" is an agenda much too large to be carried solely by the Bible experts among us. We're not saying it's not important for adults to teach the Bible to student leaders. In fact, we've found that this is a key role for adults to play in the development of student leaders. But Scripture suggests that we can learn a lot about how to obey by taking a long look at the little children around us (Matthew 18:3). Our obedience is worked out in the various situations of our individual lives—our family dinner tables, recreational softball leagues, class breaks, and endless other situations. The most effective teaching for that kind of obedience is a form of life-coaching, or showing each other how to live. There are lots of biblical "one anothers," making it clear that God expects us to teach each other naturally, "while going." Students will discover the courage needed to be people of integrity because they see their friends stand straight when it's easier to cave in. These student-leader models often aren't flashy, but they certainly are effective. They also line up nicely with one of the major ways the New Testament instructs us to teach one another.

Adults should be clear-minded about how the first goal of student leadership is to develop these exceptional teenagers into mature and faithful followers of Jesus Christ. The task of peer evangelism will flow naturally from student leaders' healthy relationships with the Lord. Teenage evangelism is, after all, *their* assignment.

Be Caring Enough to Inspire

Have you ever wondered how this personal commitment thing works with kids? What forces are at work when someone decides to follow Christ-in-you? It's fascinating to see how Jesus inspired his dedicated following by first of all offering his life and example to his disciples. He pioneered a servant-leader selflessness that won the hearts of his team. He shared every part of his life with the twelve, and by doing so, imprinted an example that would forever stamp the love of God in their lives.

In our research we were able to listen to groups discuss their motivation for becoming student leaders. The teenagers in our study repeatedly identified the inspirational example of the youth worker in leading the group. These adults were out front, showing their teenagers what was expected. In fact, our research team commented frequently that a youth ministry seemed to take on the personality of its youth worker. These adults were clear in their ministry philosophies, operated confidently with their leadership teams, designed the programs for the groups, and created the atmosphere for youth-ministry gatherings. And they were deeply appreciated for their efforts.

Students who indicated that the youth minister was most helpful to their personal faith sharing (22.5 percent) came from homes where evangelism was most likely never being modeled. In fact, 80 percent of the students surveyed had either never or seldom seen a parent tell someone else about Christ. Only 3.5 percent cited their parents as most influential in their efforts to share their faith with others. While this may not mean their parents didn't do evangelism, it *does* mean students weren't seeing it. It's significant to note that these students were being asked, as student leaders, to engage in a Christian practice they had not grown up observing as a value in their parents' lives, even though the majority of them had grown up in Christian homes.

Those few students who cited parents as the most helpful to their efforts in peer outreach reported seeing their parents share their faith with *their* friends almost monthly. For these students, those windows of observation played a huge role in helping them reach their friends for Christ.

The impact of modeling, done so powerfully by Jesus among his disciples, is reflected even more significantly in another of our findings. Those student leaders who saw an adult (non-parent) share his or her faith with someone weekly or more often *themselves* reported helping more than eight friends make a commitment to Christ. If the chance to see adults in evangelism dropped to just monthly, then the student leaders most likely helped fewer of their friends (four to eight) make a commitment to Christ. Our research showed this to be a consistent trend. *The more often adults were observed sharing their faith with others, the more often student leaders shared their faith with their own friends.* When adults engaged in observable evangelism practices less frequently, student leaders followed their pattern. So those students who reported seeing adults only occasionally—if at all—doing evangelism also were likely to indicate that they hadn't helped anyone come to Christ.

One final word needs to be said about the impact of modeling before leaving this significant research finding. Students who saw *other students* lead peers to Christ were dramatically more effective in their own evangelism efforts than those who didn't benefit from such examples. Of the students who had helped friends make commitments to Christ, 85 percent said they had seen an adult do so, and 85 percent of *those* students had seen a teenager help another teenager come to Christ. *All the students who were in the most effective category in helping friends commit to Christ had seen other teenagers help friends come to Christ.* Student leaders who are effective in evangelism certainly follow modeled behavior.

So which is it? Should adults model evangelism or should teenagers? Yes! As crucial as it is for adults to model outreach, it is equally important that they do so with an eye toward developing models who ultimately will prove *most* influential: student leaders.

After such encouraging reports, you might be surprised to learn that even the top student leaders identified fear as the number one obstacle to their evangelism efforts. Fear can undermine even the sharpest youth worker's planning and training. James shared in an interview what it would have taken to "open the door" to share his faith with a peer. He was fearful because he didn't want to alienate the friend and be rejected. He went on to list all the evangelism training in which he had participated with his youth ministry. "At every monthly meeting we go out to share in teams. Once you learn how to share, it's your own [your faith becomes your own]." Later in the interview, James described the role a mission trip had played in his life. "I learned how to serve. I love being behind the scenes." This student had skills and experience, and he had seen others share their faith with friends, but had never personally played a key role in helping a friend come to Christ. The main obstacle for him was his fear.

While it's important to teach students how to explain their faith, adults would be wise to devise ways that help student leaders move past their fears of sharing Christ with others. Simply challenging teenagers to become overcomers through inspirational talks are likely as short-lived as a coach's locker-room speech at halftime. Initial enthusiasm withers quickly in the face of hulking opponents who want to hurt you. Adults need to choose long-term strategies that help their student leaders acknowledge but not be paralyzed by their fears. We need to recognize that we can very likely help students move through their fears when we model courage ourselves. Kent is one youth worker whose effectiveness as an adult model comes in part because he knows the fear of rejection and won't let it deter him from doing evangelism. Bravery inspires bravery.

Did you ever wonder how the disciples overcame their fears? We know they had them, yet the contrast between their fearfulness in the Gospels and their boldness in Acts is striking. How powerful it must have been to be eyewitnesses of the greatest act of sacrifice humanity has ever known! They understood the real fears of Jesus reflected in his prayer in Gethsemane the night he was arrested. The Apostle John must have had the image-example of our Lord Jesus in mind when he wrote, "There is no fear in love. But perfect love drives out fear" (1 John 4:18a).

Adults who share their lives and examples with their student leaders will find themselves inspiring commitments from those same teenagers. As this transformational life exchange takes place, it's perfectly natural for teenagers to look toward those adults who have become "significant others" when they need resource support for the task of sharing their faith. That's one way Kent (identified above) keeps busy sharing the gospel with teenagers. His student leaders know they can trust him if they bring their friends to him to hear about Jesus. Thus, adults demonstrate their caring in yet *another* way by making themselves available to assist student leaders by explaining Christ to their friends.

As we'll learn in chapter 5, students in our study who seldom invited their friends to talk to adults about Jesus didn't reach as many of their friends for Christ. When students more frequently invited non-Christian friends to talk to an adult, they were likely to see their friends commit to Christ. These students see adults as partners in their evangelism enterprise, a view no doubt inspired by the loving, sharing initiative visible in these adults' lives.

There is an intersection of effectiveness that can be explored when our research results are considered in light of biblical truth. Modeling works because it reflects a significant reality about how we learn. It shouldn't surprise us to see Jesus employing this truth. He appointed the twelve to "be with him" as they learned to preach the gospel (Mark 3:14). Disciples of Jesus are ultimately those people who follow him—and other exemplary models—toward Christlikeness. While it's clear that Paul wanted to help people copy Christ (Philippians 2:5), it's important to see that he offered himself as an accessible—though imperfect—pattern to help them on their way (1 Corinthians 11:1; Philippians 3:10-14; 4:9). Paul even gushed about the far-reaching impact of his modeling among the Thessalonians (1 Thessalonians 1:5-9). We adults can help inspire such a following by caring deeply for our student leaders. If, like Paul, we "press on" in our own faithfulness to Jesus, the investment we make in teenagers by sharing our very lives with them will help them step up to new—and rewarding—levels of commitment.

Adults should accept the responsibility of being significant, and initial, models of evangelism faithfulness to their student leaders. By doing so, adults will demonstrate how to overcome fear in presenting the gospel and inspire imitation. Eventually, they must be willing to yield the primary modeling responsibility to emerging student leaders who, because of modeling dynamics, will be *exponentially* more effective at reaching teenagers than adults ever could be. Finally, adults must present themselves as available resources to developing student leaders who exercise initiative by asking their friends to talk to someone other than themselves about Jesus.

Be Close Enough to Inspect

As we adults come alongside our student leaders, we can get an up-close perspective on what they need and are ready for spiritually. Jesus gained such insight with his disciples because he lived with them. He knew, for example, that they weren't ready to deal with the forecast of his upcoming death until they understood better who he really was (Matthew 16:13-21). Peter's reaction demonstrated even then that the Lord still had his work cut out for him in preparing the disciples for what was to come (Matthew 16:22-23). Most of us won't have that kind of "life together" opportunity with our student leaders. What can we do to ensure that we're close enough to inspect their spiritual progress?

Our study showed that regular accountability meetings with adults not only help student leaders grow, they also lead to greater success as students try to influence their friends for Christ. The majority of students who were effective in evangelism met regularly with adults; those who reported having no impact on their friends coming to Christ did not. During these meetings, adults got to know students while offering general guidance in the Christian faith. It was also likely that these mentoring adults would use the time to probe specific areas of student leaders' lives and pray with them. As an aside, we also found that if students had these same types of meetings with their parents, the impact was not as significant. This may be because the nature of the meetings with parents focused on informal opportunities for nurture and care rather than those more intentional meetings organized to accomplish a youth ministry's focus.

With the exception of those students who had helped more than eight friends make commitments to Christ, youth ministers were rarely the adults identified as leading these one-on-one times. Regardless of the form the mentoring meeting takes, the influence adults have in the lives of the students by meeting with them reportedly helped them to grow in their relationships with Jesus Christ and lead their friends to become Christians.

Notice that the role of these adult "coaches" in the lives of students is focused not on evangelism task performance, but on life growth and accountability. As we discussed in the previous chapter, our focus with student leaders ought to be person-centered disciple-making. This doesn't mean evangelism coaching is *not* part of this natural accountability structure. On the contrary, students who were coached at least monthly on how to share their faith were dramatically more effective in reaching their peers than those who did not receive such a benefit. However, this evangelism coaching was done in the context of a larger purpose to become faithful in all of life, not just skilled in a particular task.

One of the practical ways "in your life" coaching and life assessment can be launched is through retreats and mission trips. Teenagers in our study consistently identified such time-intensive experiences with adults as real milestones in their Christian life. This should be no surprise. One of the reasons for the effectiveness of wilderness camping and other such events in ministry is that raw experiences help strip away pretense and expose the true depth of one's character. An astute adult walking alongside a young woman who has been sufficiently humbled by a mission trip's challenges is in the best position to see her needs for Christian growth and respond insightfully. Good coaches know their teams well and craft their strategies accordingly.

As we adults draw near to our student leaders, we will inevitably be in a position to influence how they use their time. Should student leaders focus their limited energy on managing and planning youth ministry programs? Our findings suggest that this is a role best left to adults. We are committed to the idea that students ought to be ruthless in their focus, aiming to grow in their maturity and faithfulness to Jesus Christ. Feedback and planning in youth ministry are important aids to adult leaders, but they shouldn't be the focus of the student-leader team. Most of the groups in our study centered their ministries around a philosophy similar to "Love God, Love Others, Love the Lost." The research team heard different versions of that phrase at quite a few sites. Groups who were highly concerned about honoring God, about their love for each other, and about reaching out to those who didn't know Jesus were effective in reaching others for Christ. This evangelism effectiveness dropped off among those groups who asked their best teenagers to invest themselves in directing the *programs* of youth ministry.

The truth is that there was virtually no relationship between having students help plan events and any specifically evangelism-related behaviors. Further, program planning seemed unconnected to other spiritual benefits. Helping plan events didn't even correlate with being involved in church in any significant way! If student leaders spend much time planning events, there is less likelihood that they'll fall into the category of student leaders who reach more friends for Christ, pray more, or are more involved in their churches.

So while we adults should always be on the lookout for ways to increase the confidence of our student leaders through responsible delegation, it doesn't follow that program planning and management is a good investment of time for our teenagers. We contribute to the trust bond that exists between us and our student leaders when *we* provide programming that helps them have confidence that as they invite others, the meetings will be socially safe and relevant to the world where teenagers live.

Let's be clear. We're not advocating that student leaders stay away from programs. But we have to free student leaders from unnecessary, energy-diffusing burdens. We want to help student leaders concentrate their focus. When we ask them to invest significantly in program leadership, we may do so at the expense of their effectiveness in evangelism.

How should student leaders learn what is expected of them? The youth workers in our study took initiative to be clear in communicating those expectations. These adults also used the Bible to teach students what God expects of them. This finding tips us off to yet another key role adults are to play in developing student leaders.

In our study, every group visited reported that adult leaders supplied strong Bible teaching for their student leaders. Not only that, but student leadership was well-organized and purposefully designed to accomplish all the ends described here—including Bible study. The organizational efforts of these groups were striking. The stable, established structures provided a consistent environment where adult staff and student leaders knew their roles and where effective, purposeful teaching took place on a regular basis.

Was there any pattern to the Bible content learned? We heard three predominant biblical teaching themes from the students in our study as they reported what they had learned from their adult leaders. The first theme was the challenge to demonstrate purity and integrity. They were taught that an obedient life needed to be demonstrated in their friendships, their dating relationships, and their decision-making. A second theme was to urge students to boldly go and share the good news of Christ. It reinforced the reason why these groups were successfully reaching other teenagers. They taught that evangelism is important in a myriad of ways. The third theme was that teenagers should allow God to work in their lives by practicing the kind of self-denial Jesus asked of his followers.

These certainly aren't the only biblical teaching themes worthy of student leadership. In fact, a number of youth workers reported that their teaching focus was on the character of God and how to worship God. They felt it was important to call these core groups of students to be with the One who had called them to reach others.

No doubt this reinforces the prayer emphasis we discovered to be so characteristic of fruitful ministries. One youth worker wanted his student leaders to approach this Bible teaching as a time when they could "let God continually refine your life."

> Adults should understand and expand the levels of trust student leaders have for them through weekly coaching-accountability structures, consistent Christ-honoring programs, and confidence-building delegation.

Sure, adults need to teach student leaders from the Bible, but how should we determine what should be taught? We'll best make those decisions when we're close enough to our student leaders that we can inspect their "gaps" in maturity and faithfulness. Armed with these insights, it's pretty simple to teach toward their most immediate learning needs.

Adults should understand and expand the levels of trust student leaders have for them through weekly coaching-accountability structures, consistent Christ-honoring programs, and confidence-building delegation. In addition, adults should take advantage of experientially powerful events such as retreats and mission trips to observe the learning levels of Christian integration that have taken root in the lives of their student leaders. Finally, adults need to provide a regular diet of instruction from God's Word that will help student leaders grow in their maturity as they grow in understanding biblical truth and God's expectations for their lives.

Be Challenging Enough to Influence

Teams of student leaders can be powerful vehicles to help students more effectively reach their friends for Christ. Significant influence is possible when a group of students is dedicated to impacting their friends and schools for Jesus Christ. In the groups we researched, adult leaders paid close attention to their most important values and then organized structures that effectively held the groups accountable to those values. Obviously, evangelism faithfulness was one such common value among the groups we studied. Forming a core leadership group also seemed to be a crucial part of each group's "master influence plan."

We also noticed that the groups were well-set up to receive and act upon challenges to increase their faithfulness, especially with regard to reaching out to others. Group members seemed to support one another in risk-taking. Creativity was their standard as they brainstormed ways to meet new opportunities for evangelism. They rarely seemed to shrink from the next challenge. For these healthy student-leader teams, the question was seldom "Should we?" but more commonly "How should we?" One group drama- tized the liberation of this type of thinking when they asked, "How should we spend a week together in the summer?" rather than assume that they would simply go to the camp they always attended. This openness led them to explore possibilities that included evangelism. By the time their youth director suggested that they should try to influence a small town for Christ by taking their "camp" into the community for a week, the team was eager to respond to the challenge.

Didn't Jesus capture the imagination (and hearts!) of his followers by calling them to great acts of faith? "You give them something to eat," he told the disciples when they won- dered if it wasn't time to send the large crowd away so they could grab some grub (Mark 6:37). He invited Peter to join him for a water surface stroll when the brave fisherman showed interest in taking the plunge (Matthew 14:29). Zacchaeus responded to Jesus' wild challenge to radically alter his lifestyle when he announced his new wealth distribution plan at dinner (Luke 19:8). Instance after instance in the Gospels illustrates that Jesus stretched his fol- lowers continually, challenging them to become what they never had dreamed possible.

The adults we saw in our study realized how creative challenges powerfully shaped the lives of student leaders. Being clear-minded about their goals; having inspired trust through their caring, open lives; and knowing their student-leader teams as only people who walk among others can; their challenges were wonderfully placed. They were just far enough out of reach to stretch their teenagers' faith, but not so far that they might dis- courage responsiveness.

Adult leaders in our study often chose evangelism training methods that felt like such a stretch to the students involved. Kids got bumped out of their comfort zones while learning how important outreach is. Those who seemed to be most effective selected training efforts that would help kids develop their skills in sharing their faith verbally. For most of us, talking to non-Christian friends about Jesus falls into the "challenge zone." It's not surprising that as students grew in their ability to explain to friends how to have a relationship with Jesus, they experienced success in seeing their friends become Christians. Evangelism Explosion and Dare 2 Share were two programs frequently identified by ministries in this research project as vehicles they use to train students in verbal faith-sharing skills. These training efforts—while offered regularly—usually took place at a time distinct from both the main youth meetings and the student-leader team meetings. The success these students and ministries realized in seeing teenagers commit to Christ was significantly attributed to this "extra" training. Calling students to step up to this new level of participation was clearly a challenge.

We shouldn't lose sight of the importance of challenging student leaders to do more (when they aren't doing enough) or to do better (when their effort is poor). If we have a clear picture of what student leaders can become in Christ; if they know we care about them and, therefore, trust us; and if we're close enough to understand what they need most in their next step of growth; it's wrong for us *not* to seek to influence them. This adult role is well-done—almost naturally done—by those people who help develop students for effective leadership among their peers.

Remember also that Jesus was especially adept at delivering challenges to his disciples through appropriate delegation (he knew what they were ready for) and sensitive problem-posing (he stretched them to expand their understanding, not to embarrass them). We'll be smart if we learn more about our Lord's style as we work with our student leaders.

Adults should stay alert to the transformational power of their student leaders' natural life agenda so they can challenge students to greater depth, provoke students to deeper reflection, and stimulate students to more thorough integration. It's abundantly clear that this type of influence by adults will not take place if there is not a shared life context that encourages ongoing life accountability.

Our research uncovered some sharply defined roles and activities that wise adults will engage in if they want to be genuinely helpful in equipping students for evangelism effectiveness. Among those insights were the following:

- Adults should model evangelism-related behavior.

- Adults should provide dependable programs of quality.

- Adults should make themselves available to talk with spiritually curious teenagers.

- Adults should teach the Bible.

- Adults should organize student-leader development and evangelism opportunities.

- Adults should train student leaders in evangelism skills.

- Adults should meet at least weekly for accountability with student leaders.

As a further implication, we may need to multiply the number of adults involved in our youth ministries. (For example, very few adults

> Adults should stay alert to the transformational power of their student leaders' natural life agenda so they can challenge students to greater depth, provoke students to deeper reflection, and stimulate students to more thorough integration. It's abundantly clear that this type of influence by adults will not take place if there is not a shared life context that encourages ongoing life accountability.

in our study met weekly with more than two student leaders.) These observed activities fit nicely with the four biblical principles of disciple-making used to organize this chapter. Next we'll turn our attention to learning how the most influential student leaders focused *their* efforts. We're awfully glad that, similar to what we presented in this chapter, the findings of the next three chapters square with timeless biblical truths.

Sorta gives research a *holy* potential, don't you think?

The Student Leader Three-Step

CHAPTER 4:
Praying

The Student Leader Three-Step

Watching an archaeological excavation team in action is fascinating. The careful, meticulous, step-by-step removal of dirt and inert material to search for the valuable or historic is a lesson on patience and painstaking persistence. As the sifting screen allows the dust to settle or fly away, nuggets of treasure can unexpectedly surface at any point. Zoom the camera in on the diggers' faces at the moment of discovery, and their sense of satisfaction will be obvious.

As in excavation, research projects can surface particular treasures of insight after sifting through the piles of statistics and survey forms. From areas previously unexamined, truth that demands to be reckoned with busts into the open. Rewarding, but sobering stuff.

In a time when there are plenty of "how-to" books and seminars, we felt the need to be careful as we "sifted" through our student-leader research. Youth ministry requires a balance between the "taskness" of needed administration and the relational demands of genuinely caring for students. Since student leadership plays a key role in many student ministries, some practical questions are worth considering. While these didn't drive the design of our research, per se, we figured any insights we could come up with to help answer them would be welcome. (That's the advantage of pioneering research. *Anything* we come up with is better than the *nothing* we previously knew!)

- Should there be a distinct group of student leaders in youth ministry?
- If so, what criteria should we use to select them?
- What focus should we have as we work to develop them?
- What should student leaders focus on to reach their friends for Christ?
- Which responsibilities can/should we delegate to student leaders? Which should remain as the role of adults? Are there any that are "out of range" for kids?

• Should we use student leaders to help make our job easier? (For example, is it OK to have student leaders do mailings? set up for the weekly group meetings? wash our cars?)

• Should student leaders appear in front of their peers each week during singing or games? Or should they spend time praying each week while the youth worker leads the meeting? High-profile or behind-the-scenes?

• Is it OK to assign student leaders as the welcome committee at each youth-ministry gathering? Sort of like greeters on Sunday morning?

• Should we expect student leaders to lead small groups?

As popular as student leadership seems to be in youth ministry, surprising little has been written or taught about it. Yet most youth ministries can identify a "core group" of student leaders, even if they aren't formally designated as such. Basically, we wanted our research to contribute to the small body of knowledge in this important field.

At times the findings will simply reinforce our collective common sense. Don't let obvious, experience-confirming results lull you into complacency about the implications they may have for your ministry. The importance of particular research is often more profound than can be realized at first glance. In these findings we believe we've stumbled onto a simple elegance that may help us achieve a more streamlined economy of effort with student leaders. We tried to make the case in the first two chapters that it's important to focus our efforts in the right direction. The same is true for our student leaders. We want them to concentrate on activities that will help them tell others about Jesus. In this section we'll learn that if our student leaders *pray* creatively, *invite* others generously, and *tell* others what Jesus means to them, they'll align themselves with the most effective faith-sharing teenagers in the country. These three behaviors blasted out of the data collected in our study so clearly that we felt compelled to label it with a catchy name: "The Student Leader Three-Step."

Praying, inviting, and telling (P.I.T.) are not new thoughts. In fact, they are clearly rooted in Scripture. But their significance must not be lost because of their familiarity. In the next section we invite you to join our excavation project into student leadership excellence. Take time to dust off your prior understanding, re-examine your assumptions, and consider developing a student leadership team that has such a streamlined focus so its power is harnessed to inspire young people to give their lives to Christ.

Before you start sifting, why not ask the Lord to point out where he might have you concentrate your efforts to improve student leadership?

The First Strand

"If my people, who are called by my name, will humble themselves and pray and seek my face and turn from their wicked ways, then will I hear from heaven and will forgive their sin and will heal their land" (2 Chronicles 7:14).

Late in each year as the air grows colder and the snow begins to fly, many homeowners brave the elements to decorate home and landscape with strands of Christmas lights. This tradition can be one of the most frustrating experiences of each year. Here's how it works. Somebody digs out the lights, untangles them, tests them, and starts to hang them when three good strands are working. Of course, you can count on the lights not to work once outside and on the tree. Once they fail, the great endurance test begins. Whoever has become obsessed with this task by now will have to go bulb to bulb trying to discover which low-watt light was the culprit in the power outage. (Maybe our next research study should be to investigate whether the amount of frustration experienced in locating the bum bulb is directly related to the amount of effort involved in first hanging the lights—it sure seems to be!)

On most decorative trees, it takes at least three strands to cover all the limbs so it's worthy of an "approving look" by passers-by. If one or two strands aren't working, the tree appears lopsided and poorly decorated. It won't rise to a winter wonderland acceptable standard. Neighbors may circulate petitions to rid the neighborhood of your embarrassing effort. Carefully built relational bridges may begin to crumble before your eyes. Your reputation as a Christian could suffer irreparable damages. It's not unreasonable to expect apocalyptic results. (Decide for yourself where the exaggeration starts!) All because one stinking little twinkle light not only won't flicker, but insists on taking the rest of the strand down with it!

Just as we need three strands of lights to put the festival sparkle on a winter tree, praying, inviting, and telling are all necessary to help students reach others for Jesus Christ. If even one of these strands of activity is not in place, efforts to share faith will look lopsided and sickly.

If student leaders aren't aggressively *praying*, their inviting and telling is done in vain. The psalmist reminds us that we don't want our work to be built on human strength (Psalm 127:1).

If student leaders are diligent only in their *inviting* efforts, they'll contribute to unbalanced programmatic evangelism. Personal caring that begins in prayer will be squeezed out. The transformational love-touch, such a high value to our Lord (Matthew 5:43-48), may fade away in unimportance.

If student leaders concentrate only on *telling* others, they'll be in danger of becoming evangelism Lone Rangers. They won't develop their connection with the larger body of Christ through shared prayer (Matthew 18:19-20).

We can easily fall into the trap of trying to do ministry strictly on our human strength. The end result may be quite impressive, earning admiration and even applause. Chuck Swindoll, in *The Grace Awakening*, referred to this as the "might and power" of Zechariah 4:6. "To all who are engaged in ministry, a warning is appropriate. Every project you undertake can be accomplished your way or God's way. The energy source of human strength is impressive and logical and effective. It works! Initially, folks cannot tell the difference. A ministry built by the energy of the flesh looks just like a ministry built by the energy of the Spirit. Externally, I warn you, it looks the same. But internally, spiritually, down deep in the level of motive, you know in your heart God didn't do it; *you did it!* There is no glory vertically. And equally tragic, there is no grace horizontally."

He continues to challenge, "Rather than encouraging people to pray, to wait, to seek God's mind, and to rely on His Spirit for clear direction, this [might and power] style of leadership (I have a hard time calling it a 'ministry') abuses people, uses them for unfair advantage, bullies them if they get in the way, and discards them once they are no longer 'useful.' "

Youth ministries that routinely see teenagers reaching teenagers for Christ have also adopted a God-dependent posture that centers on prayer. The first "strand of lights on the tree," the connection to the source of power in the believer's life, is prayer. Jim Cymbala echoes this in *Fresh Wind, Fresh Fire.* "The feature that is supposed to distinguish Christian churches, Christian people, and Christian gatherings is the aroma of prayer. It doesn't matter what your tradition or my tradition is…The Bible does say, 'My house shall be called a house of prayer for all nations.' Preaching, music, the reading of the Word—these things are fine; I believe in and practice all of them. But they must never override prayer as the defining mark of God's dwelling."

Prayer Is the Key

The key practice that distinguishes evangelism-fruitful student leaders from others is their pattern of prayer. Examine the lives of student leaders who are effectively sharing their faith with others, and you will find student leaders who are praying. The moment students begin to interact with God for the sake of seeing others commit to Christ, a change takes place.

Something within and through (Ephesians 1:18-19) these students begins to grow so God can use them to help their friends believe in Jesus. One of the most concrete findings in our research dramatizes this truth. *The more often students prayed for others to commit to Christ, the more God used their outreach efforts to help their friends commit to Christ.* By giving themselves to Christ in prayer, they allowed themselves to be more effectively used by him.

Tyler represents one type of student leader we learned about in our study. He prayed only monthly for opportunities to share his faith. It also was likely that he couldn't identify any friends he had helped make a commitment to Christ. (By the way, 78 percent of the students we surveyed reported that—like Tyler—this was their pattern. They usually did this praying either at youth meetings or at student leadership meetings.)

We also met some students who were like Kristen. She prayed weekly for her non-Christian friends and opportunities to reach them. She also could report that she had played a key role in helping between one and three of her friends make a commitment to Christ.

Occasionally we'd learn about a student like Keith. This young man represents those who pray a few times each week for opportunities to share their faith. It shouldn't surprise us that these were the student leaders who were most fruitful in evangelism, playing a key role in helping four or more friends put their faith in Jesus.

Clearly, the frequency with which students prayed is important. We also learned how significant it is for students to pray as groups for others to put their faith in Christ. Group prayer was a cornerstone activity for teenagers and youth ministries who were effective in evangelism. Some groups cultivated only monthly team prayer efforts. This occasional effort did little to support the impact that members of the group had in telling others about Christ. Such student leaders reported anemic results connected to their faith sharing. On the other hand, when groups reported that they prayed together for non-Christian friends on a weekly basis, God moved through them to help their peers believe in Jesus.

Is Prayer Just All Talk?

Youth ministry, what's in it? This discussion about the primacy of prayer goes right to the heart of what we believe about which of our efforts matters the most. Fun, dynamic speaking, trips, planning, outreach events, one-on-one appointments, small groups, large groups, vision statements, building relationships, mentoring, laughing together, crying together, and friendships: Youth ministry is an amazing assortment of finding non-Christians, leading Christians, fixing the hurt, and following Christ.

In the middle of this great mixture is the moment of truth (or an encounter with Truth). Individuals come face to face with the Almighty God and interact with God for salvation, healing, and obedience. Many youth-ministry ingredients (see above) can be part of leading students to encounter God, but conviction, cleansing, and redemption require God to act on our behalf. In spite of all our attempts to understand how we leaders can more effectively help people believe in Jesus, evangelism results still need to be filed under supernatural events. And only God has the key to that room.

The following youth ministry experience is not uncommon. For a long time, a particular youth pastor watched with nagging unease as his "successful" large youth ministry grew. Lots of folks saw what he did as a model for their own ministry. His group regularly met established goals, and structures were in place to virtually guarantee an electrifying youth-ministry experience for the kids attending. And kids *wanted* to attend! The ministry had weekly outreach activities, special events, small groups, and a relevant Sunday school philosophy (no small feat these days). But something was missing. Students weren't "popping" with spiritual vibrancy and an excitement to reach others for Jesus. They weren't explosive in evangelism. The adult leadership team had trouble figuring out what was wrong. Could it be that their students weren't praying often enough for opportunities to help their friends understand the truth about Jesus?

Let's confess something here. In spite of the insightful research findings, youth-ministry organizational genius, powerful philosophy, and clearly defined expectations that *might* be pried out of this book, we are lost if God doesn't move on our behalf. We're not just talking about theological lost-ness. We are literally without a clue and helpless to bring about the transformation that must happen in people's lives unless God acts supernaturally.

Given that "duh"-level statement, how could prayer *not be* foundational to evangelism effectiveness for student leaders? Could it be that as youth-ministry leaders, we make the mistake of assuming that prayer happens? Maybe too few of us model, facilitate, orchestrate, or coach prayer to the depth that is needed. Perhaps we don't establish the prominence and routine of prayer as vital to the lives of adolescents *or* their leaders!

Why not take a few minutes now to ask the Lord if he's been trying to get your attention on this matter? He sure got ours through this project.

Wired and Tired

If your desire is to see teenagers become Christians, mature in their love for Jesus, and share their faith in Jesus with others, then a consistent prayer life is essential. This certainly runs counter to the contemporary culture of consumerism and fast-paced change. Any youth ministry that radically depends on the Lord will be different. They'll experience fresh, new depths of God and will start to crave prayer as a focus of their life together. A.W. Tozer challenges in his classic *The Pursuit of God,* "Every age has its own characteristics. Right now we are in an age of religious complexity. The simplicity which is in Christ is rarely found among us. In its stead are programs, methods, organizations and a world of nervous activities which occupy time and attention but can never satisfy the longing of the heart. The shallowness of our inner experience, the hollowness of our worship, and that servile imitation of the world which marks our promotional methods all testify that we, in this day, know God only imperfectly, and the peace of God scarcely at all."

Today we have become even more a fast-paced community, wired on caffeine and achievement and weary from the breakneck pace created by our insatiable desire to squeeze as much as we can out of every moment and dollar. If we come daily to God at all, we come to him wired and tired. We try to balance incredible amounts of activity: working, raising a family, ministering, playing, reading, Net surfing, minding our cholesterol levels, watching TV, impressing others, keeping in shape, keeping appointments with accountability partners, staying connected with extended family, answering cell phones and beeper calls, paying bills, participating in a small group or two, following our favorite sports teams, listening to the latest CDs, going to movies, talking about the new whatever-we-want-to-buy-next. No wonder God has little room to exercise his lordship in many modern lives! It's an exhausting pace, and even worse for teenage students as they add layers of intensity in their issues of acceptance, family, and academic performance.

How can we possibly find space (and show others how to find space) for God to speak amidst this bedlam? *Silence?* Extinct in many areas of life. *Reflective thinking?* Necessary, but not a priority.

Don't despair too soon. We found that there are youth ministries that help kids reprioritize life. They've created space for prayer, and they help kids wedge it into their lives. Leaders have shifted their focus, their hearts, their schedules, and their mind-sets away from "running a youth ministry" so they can intentionally and proactively cultivate the expectation of experiencing God.

We detected this new direction in two areas: the focus of the weekly programs and the comments of the youth leaders. Weekly programs were focused on solid biblical teaching and a combination of prayer and worship. While crowdbreakers, mixers, and games might have been used, these lighter program elements clearly weren't what defined the kids' weekly experience. This priority shift became crystal clear when particular youth leaders shared their thoughts with us: "Put students in the presence of the Lord for significant periods of time; don't just talk about it." "The spiritual awakening in this country will be ushered in through the powerful prayer of youth." "Avoid gimmicks. The straight but creative declaration of the truth wins kids over." In shift-

"Put students in the presence of the Lord for significant periods of time; don't just talk about it."

ing their programming focus, these youth ministries experienced a fresh freedom of God-dependence that is far more than humans could ever create.

The Posture of Prayer in Youth Ministry

"I have discovered that prayer's real purpose is to put God at the center of our attention, and forget ourselves and the impression we are making on others" (Rosalind Rinker, *Prayer: Conversing With God*).

So how does it stand that with all which has been written on prayer (how to do it, how to teach it, and why it's important) we can possibly still struggle with just "going for it" and seeing what God can do as we rely on the Holy Spirit? Campaigns such as "See You at the Pole" have helped raise our consciousness, but there is still a long way to go for a lot of youth ministries to elevate the priority of prayer. How do we move our groups and ourselves into position so God can use us to reach others? Three clear steps emerge from this study as common to those groups whose student leaders have seen their friends become Christians. They are simple behaviors, and as is true with many such uncomplicated truths, the payoff comes from the discipline of actually doing them. Youth ministries most effective in helping teenagers reach teenagers with the gospel learned that God moved powerfully as they sought God often and openly. See if you can imagine what it would take for your youth ministry to be characterized by these three descriptions.

Adult leaders put prayer at the top of their priority list. Prayer starts with modeling. When the disciples asked Jesus to teach them to pray (Luke 11:1-13), it was after they had seen their leader go off by himself to talk with the Heavenly Father. Chapter 3 highlighted the role adults must play in the lives of students who will be effective at sharing their faith with their friends. We must embrace the role of first models. We cannot live lives of hollow spirituality, propped up by our impressive and flashy ministry skills. If we truly want to develop our student leaders, we'll pray for them, in front of them, alongside them, and give them the opportunity to pray with us, for us, and alongside us. If we do it often enough, naturally enough, they'll catch on. Or they'll ask us, as Jesus' band asked him, to teach them how to pray. Wouldn't that be a thrill?

We cannot live lives of hollow spirituality, propped up by our impressive and flashy ministry skills.

Think about it. When youth workers counsel, speak, or even lead their families, praying should be present. How often does an appointment end without going to God in prayer? How many times does a committee meeting go about planning, then go to God after it's done and say, "Well, Lord, please bless these plans"? Do student leadership meetings revolve around a vital time of prayer together? Do students see youth workers and staff praying individually with students at any point in the life of a ministry week? This posture of dependency on God must be established as a natural part of our lives. From such times, and *in* such times, we engage in the battle for our non-Christian friends. Our students need to know us as people who pray ambitiously and creatively for those who don't know Christ.

Students pray with increasing frequency. Many times when a group re-prioritizes to create an emphasis on prayer, they'll spend a lot of time talking about prayer, teaching on prayer, and showing examples of prayers, but spend little time in actual prayer. At some prayer meetings, the sharing of praises and requests takes three-quarters of the allotted time, and only one-quarter of the time is actually spent praying! The best way for teenagers to learn is by watching and doing, not by listening to talks. We need to get our students involved with us in real times of prayer!

The U.S. Army knows how to teach by experience. In his book *Into the Storm,* Tom Clancy chronicles the Army's adjustments in their training through the years. Working to correct the lack of quality in the post–Vietnam War era, the Army changed its training from a published set of "directives and policies" to more "mission-focused" activity. More than just assigning reading of how to conduct warfare, "once every three months he [General Starry] required all commanders and leaders to go out on the actual ground where they anticipated they would fight. There they would explain in detail to their next-higher commander just how they intended to conduct the fight." The result was a more fully trained and extremely confident army that could react and think under pressure to accomplish its goals.

Paul reminds us of the Christian's battlefield: "For our struggle is not against flesh and blood, but against the rulers, against the authorities, against the powers of this dark world and against the spiritual forces of evil in the heavenly realms" (Ephesians 6:12). As we take students out on the rocky terrain, praying once a month for opportunities to share or even once a week at a group meeting for a friend to believe in Jesus simply isn't good enough. Prayer should become a natural part of our existence so we're able to respond appropriately no matter what may come our way. Remember Troy from chapter 1? He prayed with friends at least daily for opportunities to share his faith. Never a big, highly staged deal...just a discipline he couldn't do without.

Students have opportunities more than once a month to pray with others. We adults should facilitate such opportunities. This is a key focus in the great book by Rosalind Rinker, *Prayer: Conversing With God*. She asks, "If all this [benefit] and more is waiting for us when we pray with one another and with Him, why is it that so few persons today meet to pray together? We spend hours in time-consuming pleasant conversation. We talk for an hour on the telephone. We all know how to talk. And we talk. Why then do we find so many excuses not to talk with the Lord Jesus, and with each other in His presence?"

Painfully, she answers the question a few pages later. "The real basis for not wanting to pray with someone else (aside from not wanting to answer the call of the Good Shepherd and come under His authority and His care) is usually human pride." She encourages the reader to be real, honest, even inadequate in prayer with others. "Out of the inadequacy of your prayer, the inability to express yourself, the shame of your tears, and the urgency of your need, you meet the Saviour who understands you. You are comforted and your brother is strengthened. Out of this weakness your brother, hearing and observing that you are in no better state than he, becomes strong. He is encouraged by your so-called failures that he, too, may meet the Lord in his weakness."

Some of us need to get ahold of some change strategies here. As we move our youth ministries from program-centeredness to person-centeredness, we need to be reminded that we have no greater personal need than cultivating a healthy relationship with God. Prayer is central to such a relationship. One group involved in this study deliberately set out to make this important change. Their posture is worth learning from. They focused their energy on expecting God to work in their midst and to use them to bring others into God's family. The group stepped away from the need to always play games, trying to impress, and living in fear of "going for it" in evangelism. They simply tried to focus on God together. What an adventure!

Don't look for a quick fix in the pages describing this research. A ministry that facilitates adults' involvement in teenagers' lives and emphasizes meeting God in prayer takes a lot of work. Being faithful to truth is worth the effort even when it challenges other long-standing values or methods that have been held dear. It can be scary and dangerous to change youth-ministry practices, but if we come to God in our inadequacies, admitting our need for him and his direction and leading, it can be the greatest Christian adventure of all.

The Danger of Praying for Others to Become Christians

There is a danger in prayer, especially when prayer is focused on seeing others come to belief in Jesus. Of course we need to pray for others to believe in Christ, but prayer's essential focus must always be God, not what we want God to do for us. Seeing prayer as simply another step in getting something done changes the very nature of our relationship with God. Prayer will be "exhibit A" of our self-centered spirituality instead of the evidence of our self-abandonment to God and God's purposes.

> Of course we need to pray for others to believe in Christ, but prayer's essential focus must always be God, not what we want God to do for us.

It's important to weigh the implications for prayer and evangelism. While we're commanded to ask (Matthew 7:7-8; 21:22; John 14:13-14; 1 John 5:14), we're also reminded to "remain" in Christ (John 15:7) as we ask. Jesus further stated that not everyone who talks to God or even prophesies will enter the kingdom of heaven (Matthew 7:21-23). Rather, the final criterion is based on whether God really "knows" us. In the midst of our emphasis on prayer for the purpose of evangelism, we dare not forget the prayer's nonnegotiable priority: *friendship with God.*

Prayer Is Big...Really Big

While talking with youth ministries participating in our research project, we commonly asked if they would like to tell us anything important about themselves that they might fear could be missed by our data collection methods. In one group a young man jumped on the opportunity quickly, declaring, "Prayer is big." It sure is. It's the possibility step, the one that allows God to move in our midst. When God moves to bring about evangelism fruitfulness, the excitement is tough to contain. Student leaders experience life-changing evidence of God's activity in their lives, a reference point that can never be erased. They'll never be the same.

What have we learned from our research about how these student leaders are transformed? When they pray, their hearts change and they want to act. As they pray for God to move, these young people also wonder how God can use them to make a difference, and they invest themselves in another activity that seems critical to student-leader effectiveness. They invite others into opportunities where the truth of Jesus is shared. They also take initiative to tell their friends about the love of Jesus.

CHAPTER 5:
Inviting

How many youth workers can, *right now*, replay a tape in their memory banks of a time when they've urged teenagers to invite others into youth meetings? The student leaders most effective at evangelism do it. And then some.

These student leaders make it a priority to live openly among those they want to influence. Their *lives* are inviting; it's no wonder they also use words to draw people in. They demonstrate how Christians should live, and they combine demonstration with verbal invitations to attend youth meetings and talk with adults or themselves about Jesus.

Obviously, this is an important strategy to help students reach out to others. The act of inviting others and its relationship to evangelism effectiveness is not only intriguing, it's worthy of closer consideration. Our research indicates a direct relationship between students inviting others and their effectiveness at helping lead friends to faith in Jesus Christ. Don't miss the significance of inviting as a strategy. More than simply helping to build youth-ministry numbers, inviting can be directly linked to students putting their faith in Jesus!

In chapter 1 we pointed out that some youth ministries have an "if we build the program, they will come" philosophy. This misses the heart of personal invitation. There is plenty of inviting evidence in how God initiates his relationship with us all. "Come, all you who are thirsty, come to the waters; and you who have no money, come, buy and eat!" (Isaiah 55:1a). The prophet's words sound a lot like Jesus, don't they? "Come to me, all you who are weary and burdened, and I will give you rest" (Matthew 11:28). Look at how inviting Jesus was in the early stages of his ministry (see, for example, John 1). The parable of the great banquet is about the expanded generosity of a man's invitations in the face of others' excuses (Luke 14:15-24). The Apostle Paul exhorts us to be inviters, "We are therefore Christ's ambassadors, as though God were making his appeal through us. We implore you on Christ's behalf: Be reconciled to God" (2 Corinthians 5:20).

Inviting and Relationship-Building

Inviting friends to ministry-related functions isn't a natural occurrence in a teenager's daily relationships. Students see inviting others to youth activities as a "task" to do, sort of like a homework assignment from their youth leader. It's not uncommon to observe Christian students building relationships with non-Christians without even thinking of inviting them to youth group, telling them what Jesus means to them, or even praying for them unless prompted by someone. When youth leaders remind teenagers about inviting others, it helps them move past the main obstacles to effective evangelism (fear, busy schedule, guilt, and laziness). They begin to see themselves as critical players necessary to reach others for Jesus Christ.

This hesitancy by students to invite friends may be a surprising revelation to youth workers, but it rings true with an earlier research project done by Link Institute for DC/LA '97. Let's see if we can explain the dynamic at work. Imagine Lauren, a Christian student on a high-school campus, who spends a considerable amount of time with her non-Christian friends. They might eat together every day in the school cafeteria, talk on the phone a few times a week, even play on the volleyball team and practice together after school every day. Curious though it may be, Lauren doesn't *naturally* invite her friends to youth group. Unless it becomes a conscious thought, almost like "It's my job to invite them to youth group…here I go…" she most likely won't follow through on this task related to sharing her faith with her friends.

Many youth workers have assumed they know the problem when they frame their question, "Why aren't students building relationships with non-Christians so they can invite them?" If we zoomed back into the school to watch Lauren in action, we would see that she is already surrounded by relationships with non-Christian friends. The *task* of building relationships for the purpose of evangelism isn't necessary because those relationships are already present. Consider all the daily relational settings that are a part of her world. She sits in each of her classes with various groups of classmates, walks in the halls between classes with her closer friends, sits at the lunch table with a different group of friends, and plays sports with an even different group of friends. In the social framework of the school and her everyday life, Lauren and other Christian students don't have to work at building bridges to non-Christians; those relationships already exist!

Our role as adults is to help nudge, coach, remind, and cajole Christian students to first pray for their friends and then be deliberate in inviting them to meetings or telling them about Jesus. Close your eyes and picture one hundred student leaders, each of whom already has relationships with non-Christians. That's the reality. Now ask those to step forward who pray at least weekly for their friends to become Christians. The crowd will reduce in size quickly, but those who've emerged are likely going to be those who are effective in evangelism. From this smaller group, ask them to put up their hands if they're strategic and deliberate in inviting their friends to come into settings where they'll hear the gospel. Most, but not all, hands will go up. This smaller group will be even more fruitful in evangelism than those without their hands in the air. Can you see how this is a crucial turning point contributing to evangelism effectiveness? (By the way, that group will dwindle a little more when we ask all those who actually tell their friends about their own faith in Christ to take another step forward.)

> In the social framework of the school and her everyday life, Lauren and other Christian students don't have to work at building bridges to non-Christians; those relationships already exist!

Students who already have relationships with non-Christians need to see them as God-placed people in their world and target them for prayer, inviting, and telling opportunities. As the old saying goes, "If we all swept under our own doorstep, the world would be clean."

Inviting Is What Student Leaders Do!

What distinguishes student leaders who are effective at sharing their faith with their friends? What are the actual differences between students who have impacted their peers for Christ and Christian teenagers who haven't? Those teenagers who are most effective in peer-to-peer evangelism read the Bible no more or no less than other student leaders. They attend church activities with the same regularity as those who have never shared their faith with others, and they often hang out with church friends like every other student. They *are* different because they more frequently invite others to youth meetings. In fact, our research revealed that *inviting* is one of the two distinctive roles that our sample of quality student leaders perceived was necessary to doing their job.

One youth ministry was in a rebuilding stage when, on a particular night, a sophomore girl commented, "Why do we always put 'bring a friend' on the fliers to these events? It's like all we ever talk about is inviting others and we're not caring about those who are already coming to group." Her fear was that current attendees might not be taken care of if new kids started to come. Many Christians, not just teenagers, share this anxiety when a youth ministry starts to emphasize reaching out by inviting others.

There *is* a tension that exists when an inviting emphasis is fostered. The youth-ministry road is littered with burned-out groups where committed students seemed only to be used to pull off the next big outreach event or reach the next big attendance goal at weekly meetings. A sensitive balance is required on the youth worker's part to nurture existing attendees. That's why we wrote so passionately about a disciple-making focus in chapter 2. However, expecting student leaders to invite others isn't optional if we want students who are routinely seeing their friends come to Christ. It's no coincidence that the sophomore girl identified above had not personally invited others to that youth ministry, hadn't helped any friends come to Christ, and spent little time praying for opportunities to share Christ with her friends. If a student is inviting others, there's a good probability that he or she is also playing a key role in helping friends make commitments to Christ.

What Does Inviting Look Like?

If we can just get students to walk the halls of a school wearing sandwich boards that invite kids to their Christian groups, will they become effective evangelists? Maybe we could distribute rainbow wigs and coach kids to hand out fliers. Everyone would "know" them; wouldn't that translate into fruitful evangelism? Obviously, no.

Let's try a more reasonable suggestion. What if a student ministry concentrates its energy for one month on helping students invite their friends? Will this short-term invitation emphasis translate into effective evangelism? Perhaps. There is also the chance that it will represent an effort that doesn't fit a larger ongoing strategy. It may be just activity without value. For example, what if students become excellent inviters, but the programs they invite people to really stink? Effective inviting strategies assume that there are destinations worthy of invitations. Three specific destinations surfaced in our research as those that are commonly used by the best student leaders.

Inviting others to group meetings—Peer evangelism is most common among those youth ministries that have helped their students move from a casual rate of inviting others to weekly practices of bringing others. If never prompted in any way to invite more frequently, Christian students in our study invited a friend about once a month to their youth ministry. Not much came of this invitation usually, but it's the basic frequency at which students commonly invited their friends. On the other hand, those students who played a key role in helping friends come to Christ invited their friends to a group meeting once a week. Even more noteworthy, those students who were most successful in peer-to-peer evangelism invited friends on an almost daily basis.

The act of inviting is only part of this process. When we asked student leaders why they invited friends, the responses were insightful. "Lots of kids have become Christians here." "I became a Christian at this youth group." "I knew the message would be good." "I knew they wouldn't seem nerdy if they opened up." "The leaders devote a lot of attention to us."

The kids talked about meetings that were of a quality nature. They allowed for and facilitated an atmosphere where invitations could be rewarded by an evangelism ministry that students could be proud of. Within the ongoing plans and monthly schedule, careful attention was given to helping students invite others and providing meetings that were shaped in some way to minister to new students. Rich in biblical truth, effective discipleship, and life-changing teaching, these youth ministries still allowed room for new people to come and be involved on a regular basis. In fact, they counted on it happening. It's fair to say these group meetings were seeker-sensitive even if they weren't always seeker-targeted.

Inviting others to talk to Christian adults—As student leaders move through personal barriers to reach out to others and they talk with their friends about Jesus Christ, they often desire to involve Christian adults for help or support. This step is a significant move for student leaders. Nearly 77 percent of the student leaders in our research said they never or seldom invited a non-Christian friend to talk to an adult. If students reported that they were "teamed" with adults who were coaching them in some fashion regarding their Christian walk and witness, that relationship contributed to that student being effective at helping others make faith commitments. Those students who invited friends to talk to Christian adults on a weekly basis saw more friends become Christians because of their partnership approach to ministry.

One advantage (previously discussed in chapter 3) to this teamwork between students and adults is that the Christian student gets to watch evangelism being modeled by the adult. One student from a parachurch ministry participating in our research commented, "If I could see a gradual process of evangelism it would be encouraging." This senior girl added later, "My friends don't want anything to do with Christ and don't see the need. I don't know how to reach them." She was feeling the need for adult support to grow in her ability to reach those she cared about. To reiterate, making adults available as resources for communicating the gospel is crucial to developing student leaders who are effective in evangelism.

Inviting others to talk about what Jesus means to them—A third invitation students make to non-Christian friends is to ask them if they can talk with them personally about what Jesus means to them. Before the telling of the gospel can actually happen, an invitation to talk usually takes place. This third part of the Student Leader Three-Step, telling, will be covered in the next chapter. Of course it makes sense that those who have success sharing their faith also regularly practice the discipline of asking others if they want to talk about Jesus. For now it's important to see how seamless the relationship is between the three elements of faith-sharing effectiveness.

No Lone Rangers

Our study's focus didn't allow us to check out teenagers who may have faith-sharing success outside some sort of organized youth-ministry structure. Even so, we were prepared to find "super evangelist" students witnessing to others at the local McDonald's restaurant on a Friday night or charismatic student leaders single-handedly leading Bible study groups of over one hundred students. There are stories of students who have realized these kinds of ministries for short periods of time, but they are extremely rare, not the norm. We earnestly tried, and had the resources, to investigate the factors behind these phenomenal reports. Our search revealed that these intense experiences were short-lived, could be attributed to unusual (not common) movements of the Holy Spirit, had faded once a dynamic senior had graduated, or even that the reports of such were proved inaccurate.

There *are* some amazing students who are making incredible differences in the lives of others. These students were accomplished evangelists, and many had played a key role in more than ten of their friends becoming Christians! None of them were working on their own initiative or in their own "ministry areas," but rather within existing youth ministries that were fostered by youth workers who had created climates that encouraged students to invite others.

There were no groups exclusively populated by super kids, void of the common pitfalls that accompany youth ministry. These student-leader teams were made of ordinary teenagers, organized for an extraordinary task, committed to living in ways that would allow God to use them in any way possible to reach their friends.

The Nature of Large and Small Groups

Listen carefully at conferences, and you might hear a few youth workers talk about the pros and cons of a small-group format in youth ministry vs. one that centers on large-group meetings. The debate can get highly opinionated. "Small-groupniks" think the deeper purposes of ministry can be accomplished through their methods. "Large-groupites" are sure that a certain social luster is important in ministry with adolescents. One youth worker explained how they moved to a small-groups-only format because he wasn't satisfied with the lack of life change he saw in most of the kids attending his large-group program. Ted M. Stump echoes this sentiment: "Has God been preparing you to transition from a program-based, entertainment-oriented, adult-driven youth ministry to a relational, student-led cell model?" ("Student-Led Cell Groups: Nothing Short of a Revolution," Youthworker, September/October 1998.) Whether Stump was making an unfair generalization about large-group formats is open for debate, but there certainly are distinct characteristics of the two approaches. Let's take a look at large- and small-group formats and their impact on evangelism in youth ministry.

Those student leaders in our study participating in youth ministries with large-group orientations invited their friends to those groups much more frequently than students who were involved in a small-group format. Large groups are perceived by student leaders to be evangelism-friendly events, safe to invite their friends to. We noted that students who used large-group meetings as destinations for inviting their friends saw peers become Christians more frequently than those who didn't use large groups in this way. They also saw adults and teenagers share their faith with others within those meetings. Whatever the flaws or dangers may be in employing large groups for youth ministry, our research suggests that these settings provide one of the easiest and most helpful tools to enterprising student leaders who want assistance in sharing their faith with their friends. A forced choice between large groups and small groups doesn't seem warranted if considering the goal of youth evangelism.

The current trend in youth ministry seems to be moving toward an emphasis on small groups. Most youth ministries we visited were using a combination of large and small groups each week, but a few had committed themselves to the exclusive use of small groups. They were seeing great success, especially when measured by the incredible life change in those who attended. The potential for rich relationships and deep prayer is one of the most attractive features of a small-group ministry. Did the student leaders of our research invite their friends to come to their small-group meetings and subsequently see them become Christians? Not as often as they used large group meetings for this evangelism purpose. But each method served an important role in the overall contribution to evangelism.

To recap, student leaders using large-group meetings were more likely to invite non-Christians frequently, could observe teenagers and adults sharing their faith more often, and would intentionally build relationships with non-believers more often. They would therefore perceive these large-group settings as more helpful than small-group settings in actually reaching their friends with the gospel.

Some key things also happened when small groups were formed to advance the evangelism purposes of youth ministry. The work of prayer, already highlighted as critical to the evangelism process, clearly was best facilitated through small groups. Students prayed with others for friends to become Christians, and small groups helped people learn how to organize others for prayer. These settings also provided opportunities for a more personal style of evangelism. Adult accountability—also a critical factor contributing to student-leader effectiveness—was most clearly evidenced in small groups, and students could grow into greater degrees of confidence in their personal ministry.

The balance between overseeing a program and being person-centered (as discussed in chapter 2) requires constant monitoring. One youth minister confessed, "I just needed to seriously examine *why* I was spending so much time attempting to build programs with gimmicks and pizzazz" (Ted Randall, "Not for Mega Youth Ministries Only," Youthworker, September/October 1998). The danger, however, wasn't with the program itself, but with the way it was dominating the landscape of the ministry.

The same concern could arise in youth ministries emphasizing small groups if, for example, small groups were built exclusively upon community-building exercises, initiative games, or other "gimmicks." Youth workers who value relational ministry need to face the reality that whenever a group of people meets on a regular basis, a program is essentially born. It's imperative to lean on the Holy Spirit as we genuinely evaluate each program for its faithfulness to God's Word and its helpfulness in making us aware of the spiritual condition of the people in the group. Even in a large-group ministry, students can be spiritually healthy and vibrant.

The question is not either/or with relation to small groups/large groups or programs vs. relationships. Rather, driven by the urgent need to reach non-Christian kids and guided by the timeless principles of God's Word, we look for balances that help us do the best we can with the resources God gives us. Hopefully these insights on small groups and large groups with regard to their use by student leaders will assist in these very practical decisions.

Group Dynamics That Reach Others

The best faith-sharing youth ministries identified four distinct group dynamics as important factors to their success. Note that these are "group" dynamics and don't include elements like praying or effective planning or having a nice youth room. The qualities relate to both large- and small-group formats. It's safe to say that if these four components are evident in group meetings, there is a greater likelihood that your students will invite others with more confidence and frequency, ensuring a greater probability that their friends will come to Christ.

Meetings are socially safe. We observed that the youth ministries most effective in evangelism demonstrated an understanding of the youth culture where their students live. Each region, city, school, and neighborhood has a social framework influencing where teenagers go, what they do, how they dress, and even how they think. Where teenagers reach teenagers for Christ, this understanding is built into the design of meetings, helping students to avoid feeling awkward socially if they attend a meeting.

Youth workers who spend time with their students in informal settings can learn a lot about what's needed to ensure this safety by just listening and probing. These times are treasure chests of ministry because they not only build relationships with students, they also provide a vehicle for hearing feedback about how the youth ministry relates to the dominant social values. On a recent appointment, one high school junior said, "Oh, you're probably wanting us to come up with ways we can make youth group cooler." He was involved in a small group regularly, but he wasn't going to the large-group meeting on a regular basis. His comment was an indicator that he was thinking about the social relevancy of meetings for his group of friends.

Student leaders in our study repeatedly stressed that the social dynamics of the youth ministry were foundational to its success. While adult staff members often answered questions about their ministries' success by offering a spiritual or structural perspective, it was not uncommon for students to answer the same questions with a social orientation. Since one of the main tasks of student leaders was to invite others, their friends' opinions toward the youth ministry were highly valued.

Most student leaders were confident they could invite their friends because they knew they would be accepted well. One student summed it up, "I knew I could invite friends because I felt comfortable there." Another added, "Everyone mobbed us and welcomed us. Instead of being pushed away, I was drawn in." We can't overstress this factor's contribution to the success faith-sharing students experience. *This atmosphere of safety is so important to teenagers, it could enable or disable a youth ministry's outreach to non-Christians.* Youth workers would be wise to remember this while reminding students frequently that warm acceptance of new people should be a key part of their ongoing practices.

One youth minister wrote that it's important to "provide a balance of programming that allows a place for a youth to plug in no matter where he [or she] is spiritually." Not embarrassing students through the games or activities that take place can nurture this social safety. Crowdbreakers that have the potential for humiliating even a few teenagers would be clearly detrimental to the social safety needed by a youth ministry that is invitation-worthy for student leaders.

Terry remembers an incident from his own high-school experience that illustrates the power of social safety. It took place at an event designed to welcome incoming freshmen into a local Campus Life club in the seventies. As an incoming freshman, small in stature, he tried to dress as "in" as he could with the high-schoolers. He came to the meeting excited about this sample of Campus Life. The first game was Rat-a-Tat-Tat and Terry was asked, along with others, to come up front and play at this, his first club meeting. The game was designed so that the "lucky" participant (Terry in this case) would mirror the actions of another person as he simulated being a tail gunner on an old airplane. At one point, Terry was led to stand up and, while standing, a staff member secretly put a wet washcloth on the chair underneath him. When he sat down, he "experienced" the wet washcloth. Of course he was surprised, and everyone had a good laugh. Except Terry. As he stood up, he was embarrassed that his new cool purple corduroy bell-bottom pants now were wet. Terry put on his bravest front, but as he recalls, "I was heartbroken. I slipped quietly into a room in the back of the house whenever I could do it quietly and never went to Campus Life the rest of my high school life."

As a postscript, God has a way of using our hurts to help us fix some wrongs. Terry eventually led Campus Life clubs as a full-time employee for eight years. In his early years, he saw some kids react negatively to various stunts and remembered his own sense of humiliation in front of people who were important to him. Those games that could embarrass never were used again. (He *never* used Rat-a-Tat-Tat!)

Meetings are emotionally safe. Not only did the youth ministries in our research demonstrate they understood the need for social safety, but they took steps to ensure a kind of emotional safe-zone as well. Social relevance was never established at the cost of authenticity. Kids were free to be happy, sad, hurt, jubilant, in conflict, and even fragile. One group critiqued themselves in this area, "We invite and hug, but only when people are hurting. We need to care for each other all the time." This type of attention to the emotional qualities within each group was common among the groups where teenagers were reaching teenagers for Christ.

Meetings are consistent from week to week. Our research showed that there needs to be a dependable quality to the ongoing ministries, however that may be defined for a particular group or event. If inviting is important to students in helping their friends come to Christ, they need to be confident in their meetings. The student leaders were able to know that they could count on quality each week from their youth ministries. There was enough consistency and familiarity to their meetings that student leaders knew what they were inviting their friends to. Imagine what would happen if there was inconsistency. A student might invite a friend thinking it was going to be a Bible study like last week, and instead it was a "battle of the classes" competition designed for underclassmen. Worse yet, what if the ministry purposes might change from semester to semester as the latest book or convention entirely re-shaped the thinking of the youth worker? It's not hard to see why consistency is an important asset to provide student leaders who are asked to invite others to their youth ministry's meetings.

Meetings are appropriately Christian in nature. A student had just returned from spending considerable time checking out a well-known youth ministry. She was unimpressed. "If it weren't for the opening prayer, I couldn't tell it was a Christian student-leader group." Hopefully the two characteristics of social relevance and "appropriately Christian in nature" are not perceived as polar ends of a spectrum, incapable of coexisting in a particular youth ministry. Those groups realizing peer-evangelism success managed to be distinctly Christian in nature while maintaining a commitment to social relevance. This was integral to the success of the effectiveness of their student leaders.

Since these groups held evangelism in high regard, it wasn't surprising to see that the youth ministry facilitated students' efforts to share their faith with their friends. In many cases, the expectancy was clear: Students were accustomed to seeing teenagers become Christians at their youth meetings. In fact, for many groups the "appropriately Christian" aspect was the weekly presentation of the gospel, including an open opportunity for student responses.

In all four of these important factors, it's important not to make them legalistic. If that happens, we lose the heart of our ministry. Don't lose the main point here: Student-leader *confidence* in inviting friends is significant rather than the particular components or characteristics of the group. Do the students have confidence in the social and emotional safety of the group, that it will be consistent in style and purpose, and that as they invite their friends it will be a place that is appropriately Christian? Paying attention to these areas will aid the efforts of students as they share their faith with their friends.

Final Inviting Thoughts

As we listened to these effective student leaders, it quickly became clear that they had reached two common milestones in their lives. First, their heart focus had changed.

These groups loved non-Christians for who they were. They chose words to describe their group like "accepting," "welcoming," and "understanding." They revealed a change from an "us" orientation to a focus on others. They considered their attention to outreach to be an integral part of their youth ministry. It was far more than a youth pastor hot button; all the student leaders were involved.

The second milestone was their adoption of a common goal to move past typical outreach barriers and into the cooperative mission of helping others make a commitment to Jesus. Evidence of these goals sometimes took tangible forms, with phrases like "Be bold!" or "Get out of your comfort zone" trumpeted about. (Our favorite was "Teachers don't make seating charts, God does.") These were used as reminders of the task they had before them to become people who help others come to faith in Jesus Christ.

There's plenty to reflect on in this chapter as you consider how well (and how often!) your student leaders invite their non-Christian friends into settings where they can be exposed to the hope of Jesus. Are adults readily available as resources for faith-sharing conversations? Do meetings measure up to the kinds of standards that give student leaders confidence as they risk inviting their friends? Are there increasingly creative ways you can assist student leaders as they take inviting initiatives with their peers? (Maybe you can ask them what invitation-worthy programs or activities would help them reach their friends. When a Florida youth minister asked that question, it led the church to develop a skateboard park and batting cages on the church's property!) Eventually we want our student leaders to develop the greatest confidence as possible as they *tell* their friends about Jesus!

CHAPTER 6:
Telling

For students and adults alike, the skill of clearly sharing the words of the gospel is tough to master. Even as students pray for others to become Christians and invite them to youth meetings, the gospel still has to be expressed verbally. If we want student leaders to be able to share the good news, then obviously we should help them learn how to do that. It didn't take long in our research before we realized that *youth ministries who see teenagers help teenagers become Christians work diligently to prepare their student leaders in the telling art.* Personal evangelism was an observable value in almost all these youth ministries.

Training students to be verbal witnesses is sometimes lost amidst emphases on Christian discipleship and nurture, but being a verbal witness is the central method God has chosen to spread the good news of Jesus Christ (2 Corinthians 5:11-21). Jesus called the disciples to follow him and said he would make them fishers of men (Mark 1:17). The Apostle Paul even wrote, "Woe to me if I do not preach the gospel," adding later that he desired, "to win as many as possible" (1 Corinthians 9:16b, 19b). The disciples had spent rich time with Jesus. It is no wonder they couldn't keep from telling others about Jesus' grace and forgiveness even in the face of persecution and impending death.

Robert E. Coleman, in the classic book *The Master Plan of Evangelism,* writes about Jesus' objective, "The days of His flesh were but the unfolding in time of the plan of God from the beginning. It was always before His mind. He intended to save out of the world a people for Himself and to build a church of the Spirit which would never perish." Today's student leaders are key players in this master plan from the heart of the Lord Jesus.

When students take a bold, even rare, step to actually share the gospel, supernatural things can happen. If students tell others about Jesus, our research shows that they've also likely been praying regularly, reading the Bible almost daily, and memorizing Scripture to help their efforts. "Remember that the Holy Spirit is working behind the scenes to convince the non-Christian that every symptom can be traced to the root problem of unbelief in

Christ (John 16:8-11). Wherever the gospel is proclaimed in all of its purity and simplic-ity, Jesus is surely at work" (Mark McCloskey, *Tell It Often—Tell It Well: Making the Most of Witnessing Opportunities*).

Should we expect that every student will become adept at sharing his or her faith? Even in youth ministries where teenagers regularly reached other teenagers for Christ, sharing the good news wasn't natural for student leaders. When asked how often they explained to friends how to begin a relationship with Jesus Christ, nearly half the students participating in our study said it never or seldom happens. Remember that this response was from stu-dent leadership groups with a track record for evangelism success! Another third added that they share the gospel details with friends about monthly. Clearly, the "telling burden" in these effective youth ministries was carried by slightly less than 29 percent of their students, who reported that they were verbally sharing their faith more than once a month.

Sometimes the role of research is to dispel myths created by reputations. When we searched out youth ministries with strong reputations for peer-to-peer evangelism, we imagined that two-thirds of the students were regularly active in sharing their faith. So when half the student leaders in our study reported that they seldom shared the gospel, we became instantly curious. Do their fears play such a big role that they're hindered from sharing? Is the boldness to tell others about Jesus just a natural byproduct of the matura-tion process? If that's the case, we should be able to see from our research that older stu-dents share more frequently than younger students. Is it even realistic to expect that a majority of our students will tell their friends how to have a relationship with Jesus?

As central as telling is to reaching others for Christ, these typical students clearly are not wild-eyed evangelists.

The Typical Student Leader

What profile emerges from our research to describe the typical student leader from these atypical student ministries? Let's look at some clear findings. The typical student leader in these youth ministries...

- has played a key role in one to three friends becoming Christians.
- most likely became a Christian with the help of a parent or another key family member.
- reads the Bible a few times a week, but not quite daily.
- thinks the most important thing to do as a leader is to encourage others.
- cites fear and being too busy as the biggest obstacles to overcome in sharing faith with friends.
- identifies youth workers and friends as his or her biggest helps in telling others about Christ.
- invites friends to youth meetings a little more than once a month.

Regular Training

When training in evangelism took place frequently, student leaders moved forward in their ministry development. Youth ministries effective in evangelism carry out regular training efforts—be they formal or informal in nature—to help students learn how to tell others about Jesus. Even if student leaders have been active in only the first two steps (praying and inviting), there is still the strong possibility that they'll get a chance to verbally share with a friend. The training efforts focused on the need to be ready—to know what to say and how to say it. The groups in our study wanted their students to know how to tell others about Jesus. As a common value, they also regularly promoted the need to be ready to tell.

So how often is "regular"? What kind of priority should be placed on evangelism within a youth ministry? How often in the schedule of a youth ministry should youth workers teach student leaders how to share their faith? Can we put too much emphasis on evangelism? We certainly agree that there are ministries with a strong commitment to outreach that is practiced in unhealthy, unbalanced ways. In fact, given that each of the groups in our study had excellent ministry reputations, we were surprised by how *much* emphasis these groups put on evangelism. It reminds us that balance does not necessarily have to result in an equal division of time or energy. We believe the deliberate evangelism concentration we found among the groups in our study contributed to the result of teenagers reaching teenagers for Christ.

There was a real difference in the practices of student leaders who were coached more than once a month on how to share their faith. This was one of the most significant findings in the statistical returns from the research. If evangelism training took place monthly, the impact on the evangelism efforts of the student was average or minimal. However, if that coaching moved to more than once a month, there was a notable increase in how many students became Christians because of their efforts. This more-than-once-monthly "coaching" was accomplished through a combination of focused discussions (at student-leader meetings), regular youth training (another night of the week), and adult mentoring with evangelism as a point of interaction. Taken together—and accompanied by the modeling power of witnessing adults—these supplied a constant rhythm of reminders and instruction about verbal evangelism.

An interesting observa-
tion we had as we met
with youth ministries
was how the student-
leadership group re-
flected the personality of
the youth leader. We
could see in a short visit
that teenagers had taken
on their leader's personality, behaviors, values, and
even sense of humor!

Model Evangelism

Modeling evangelism proved to be one of the best ways to train others how to share their faith. An interesting observation we had as we met with youth ministries was how the student-leadership group reflected the personality of the youth leader. We could see in a short visit that teenagers had taken on their leader's personality, behaviors, values, and even sense of humor! It was no surprise to see that adult leaders of the youth ministries in this project incorporated evangelism in their lifestyles. Students emulated what they saw in the lives of their leaders. The leaders were convinced of the importance of sharing their faith and wanted to see that in their student leaders' lives as well.

One youth pastor took his students along with him on faith-sharing appointments with his peers. His hope was that they would learn even more about sharing their faith when they saw *his* nervousness and strategy as he did his own peer-to-peer evangelism. He wasn't just living a life of outreach with teenagers so his youth ministry would do evangelism, he was presenting the gospel to his friends, and he wanted his teenagers to catch his heart for non-Christian friends.

There is a very significant point to be pressed here. Some ministries have considered evangelism to be a set of skills that can be trained for. We're convinced that evangelism is at least as much a *value* as it is a combination of trainable abilities. So while skills might be learned through demonstration and lecture, values need to be modeled if they will be picked up. That's why it's true that more is caught than taught with regard to equipping students for evangelism.

Students reported that their youth leaders, other student leaders, the youth program, and training times were all most helpful to them as they learned evangelism. A noticeable absence from this list was parents. The parents of students in our research had not modeled evangelism very well to their children. More than 80 percent of the student leaders said they had never or seldom seen their parents lead someone to Christ. In fact, parental influence was a non-factor in our findings overall—except at the students' original moment of conversion, which usually took place in childhood.

What happened from childhood on the way to adolescence? Only 3 percent of the students pinpointed their parents when asked to describe what was most helpful in their peer-evangelism efforts. Youth leaders were asking their students to engage in evangelism, a Christian discipline they hadn't grown up observing as a value in their parents' lives, though most of these student leaders grew up in Christian homes. This outreach mentality and lifestyle were things they were being introduced to for the first time as they entered a youth ministry. An important logical progression can be observed here. If most people who become Christians do so by the age of eighteen, it may be that their best hope for becoming faith-sharing adults is through the experience of student ministry in high school or college-age years.

Given this responsibility to train students how to share, the importance placed in Scripture on our role as God's "ambassadors" (2 Corinthians 5:20), and the success of modeling as a training method, youth workers need to deliberately design ways for students to "catch" evangelism from others. Issler and Habermas describe two forms of modeling: structured and spontaneous. Structured Modeling provides "a regular standard for emulation" and takes the form of classroom features like lecture, dramatic scenes, movies, role plays, and moments where purposeful demonstration is orchestrated. "Spontaneous Modeling is not planned—it just happens. It is characterized by how we live our lives before others, how we respond to various circumstances of life. What do we say and how do we react to a flat tire, spilled coffee, or a 'C' on a final exam?

"The contribution of Spontaneous Modeling to learning is that we can observe positive expressions of faith in the lives of others. We represent living 'commentaries' of the truth. We answer the question: 'What does God's truth look like in day-to-day living?'...We demonstrate the validity of what it means to be 'Christian' through our intimate relationships with God and others." (Klaus Issler and Ronald Habermas, *How We Learn: A Christian Teacher's Guide to Educational Psychology.*)

Certainly both structured and spontaneous modeling were prominent in youth ministries where evangelism took place on a regular basis. As noted in chapter 3, the students who reached more of their friends for Christ saw someone help another make a commitment to Christ almost weekly. Regular exposure to adults sharing faith with teenagers significantly influences student leaders' effectiveness in sharing faith with peers. More distinctly, if those teenagers watch other teenagers tell peers about Christ, the impact on their faith-sharing efforts is even more dramatic.

Of the students who had helped friends become Christians, 85 percent said they had seen adults tell others about Jesus, and 85 percent of that group had seen teenagers tell other teenagers about Christ. Modeling how to share the gospel is one of the most powerful training tools available to help students reach their friends for Jesus Christ. If modeling is necessary for student leader effectiveness, youth workers will need to strategize with this reality in mind.

Being an Example As Part of the Telling

The old phrase "actions speak louder than words" was never more apparent than in conversations with students about sharing their faith. Modeling for students took on the form of being a good example. It was the first consideration by most of these students as they talked about their ministry to their peers. They weren't just watching how they acted so they were faithful in their own walks with God...they were purposeful in "exampling" for others to note. When asked about it, one student quickly exclaimed, "Yes, it's important! It's the *hugest* thing!"

Being a good example to non-Christians was important to student leaders as they strove to share their faith through their actions and display the impact of their beliefs on their behavior.

We discovered that it was very important to students that they demonstrated consistency not only in their moral behavior, but also in how they related to others. Within the social framework of a school or peer group where various norms and values translate into actions, these student leaders understood the need for harmony between what they believed and how they lived. If contradictions existed between the two, unbelievers wouldn't be interested in hearing their verbal witness for Christ. There would be no authenticity to the message. Even though it may seem obvious to youth workers, this reality was a big deal to students and part of their conscious efforts to reach their friends.

The second way being an example played a key role was discovered within the structures of the youth ministries. These were student *leader* groups, and as student leader teams are formed within a youth ministry, the opinions of other students toward the teams can help or hinder the group's ability to lead. If the teams give careful attention to how they are perceived, they can experience even greater impact. For example, when asked why he was a student leader, one teenager commented, "I saw the senior guys on the leadership team and I wanted to be like them."

Team Sharing

One way many of these students learned to share their faith was through the efforts of team sharing. Mall evangelism and prayer walks were common methods that allowed students to both share their faith and watch other students in their teams as *they* told others the good news. Almost half the students in our study went out in teams to share their faith at least once a month. When other students who shared their faith joined them they were provided with valuable training on how to tell others about Jesus.

Not all youth workers are sold on the idea of a non-relational approach to evangelism. In fact, the thrust of our evangelism priority ought to take us into conversations with those who are part of our regular circle of acquaintances. We want kids to reach their friends. But on the way toward that natural goal, students often learn *telling* skills through other initiative-taking approaches to evangelism. Evangelism Explosion and Dare 2 Share are organizations that train students how to share the gospel clearly with anyone they encounter in a variety of natural contexts, like walking down the street or doing business at a store. Youth ministries used team sharing to go out in groups of two or more to share the gospel. They went door-to-door to homes of specific teenagers, to shopping malls, or along streets. Usually the people they talked to were unknown to the team before they met. After initiating a conversation or asking people to complete a survey, team members asked a question designed to create interest in listening to a (usually) quick presentation of the gospel. The number of times people have prayed prayers of commitment to Christ in such encounters is staggering.

Students reported there were few ongoing relationships after these encounters and follow-up was often nonexistent. Of course, there were exceptions. Often, individuals they shared with were adults, who would never be interested in attending youth meetings and, as a result, the group members weren't able to report how these people were doing spiritually. The claim by youth leaders who employ these methods is that team sharing might be the best way to help student leaders combine the desired skills with the required boldness to be effective in their telling. While many youth ministries live this out only on mission trips one week a year, some evangelism-committed groups push their students to practice this discipline about once a month in their own neighborhoods.

The Role of Scripture

A key distinctive of these groups was found in the centrality of the Bible to their relationships with one another. They were committed to providing clear biblical teaching each week. Their students were routinely engaged in personal devotions and were memorizing Scripture. Further, teenagers in our study reported that Scripture and biblical teaching were the main ways they knew what was expected of them as student leaders. As they studied and learned from the stories of men and women in Scripture, they discovered the truth regarding issues in their lives as Christians and as leaders. However, while Scripture was foundational to student leaders' spiritual growth and development, Bible reading did not predict evangelism activity. Even those who had never played key roles in their friends' becoming Christians had personal devotions a few times each week. While the Bible was central to the life and teaching of these youth ministries, student leaders derived their motivation to share from other previously mentioned sources.

There was, however, a significant difference in evangelism fruitfulness among students who memorized Scripture. The average student leader worked on memorizing Scripture a little more than once a month, while those who played a key role in more than four friends becoming Christians memorized Scripture regularly. The implications are that these students were not only equipped with tools, but practiced learning Scripture to use with their friends as they shared. It is very likely that their earliest experiences in sharing with others convinced them of their need for using Scripture to tell the gospel story.

The Role of Training Conferences

One method commonly marketed for use in training student leaders how to share their faith is attending a large conference that focuses on evangelism training. Any contemporary youth-ministry magazine or denominational youth mailer has advertisements for these mega-conferences. There is evidence (Link Institute's DC/LA '97 research project, August 1998) to suggest that many of these conferences effectively inspire students to share their faith and to do so more often. It was noteworthy, however, that the faith-sharing youth in this project didn't note conferences as integral to their training development. In fact, while retreats and summer camps were noted for being important historical events, large conferences were absent from the responses of the student leaders. When it came time to choose, the camps and retreats the local group attended were cited as more important to student leaders' development. Were conferences seen as effective? Sure. Did these youth ministries attend them? Yes. Were they perceived as nonnegotiable to their evangelism training strategy? No.

The Importance of Mission Trips

With startling frequency, the participants (students, adults, and youth leaders) in this research project identified mission trips as the most important historical events in the lives of their group members for developing their evangelism skills. Well-run mission trips—complete with the preparatory training involved—contributed to student leaders' effectiveness at sharing their faith. Given how teenagers learned from experience, these trips provided powerful moments of encountering God and being available to the Holy Spirit while reaching out to others.

One danger accompanying short-term mission trips is an unhealthy reliance on the naturally powerful experience and environment of the trip to do the shaping of evangelism skills. There may be little intentional thought given to the ministry purposes and practices that are appropriate and God-honoring for each group of students. John Dewey reminded secular educators in the mid-1900s, "It is not enough that certain materials and methods have proved effective with other individuals at other times. There must be a reason for thinking that they will function in generating an experience that has educative quality with particular individuals at a particular time" (John Dewey, *Experience and Education*).

A recent report from a mission trip may illustrate Dewey's point in relation to telling others about Christ. While watching a particular youth ministry in action in Romania, a missionary commented, "This group has done more in a week and a half with the street kids than I've had groups come over and do in six weeks." When asked to explain the difference, he noted the students' willingness to work, their ability to verbally share the gospel, their expression of love and care cross-culturally, their prepared plan for ministry opportunities, and the evident training they had before they went overseas. Preparation in the direction of mission effectiveness and lasting impact made the difference.

Most of the students in our study reported seeing God work through them on mission trips as they verbally shared the gospel. It became a "wake-up" time for some to commit their lives to serve God. A youth pastor once wrote, "I grew up in a pastor's home and sat through billions of mission conferences. I was mission-conferenced out of my ears, yet it wasn't until my senior year in high school that I went to Venezuela and experienced missions. I didn't go to necessarily minister—I just wanted to see firsthand what a foreign mission field was like. But it was there I got a heart for missions; it was there the Lord called me to ministry of some sort" (Interview with Paul Hansen, "Youthworker Round-table: Are Youth Mission Trips Biblical?" Youthworker, Fall 1989).

A ministry of telling provides lots of nurture and discipleship as students see God work and learn to rely on God more. When a youth ministry focuses on the important things that change lives—praying, inviting, and telling—exciting things can happen. As one student said, "God moves a lot in this youth group and that keeps me going." Another quickly added, "Knowing that each of us has a ministry God is calling us to, we know that people are hearing the gospel because of us."

If it hasn't been clear already, listening to comments like those above contributed an important richness to this study. The way groups talked together about their life with God provided the last, perhaps most intriguing, finding from our research.

Making Student Leadership Work for Youth Evangelism

CHAPTER 7:
Stages of Vitality

It was sixty-two degrees at the start of the ceremony, but the gym very quickly heated to a sticky seventy-seven degrees. Parents, friends, and faculty were packed in the high-school gym for the commencement exercises to celebrate this big day in the life of the seniors. As the graduates proudly filed across the stage one by one, Brad took the opportunity to reflect on his years of ministry with this particular class. Prompted by the nostalgia of the occasion, Brad wondered how effective the youth ministry he led had been in helping shape these students' lives.

An area of inconsistency from year to year was student leadership. Brad wanted to pour himself into students and truly mold them for ministry, but it wasn't working, or at least that was his interpretation. It seemed as if each summer he would tinker and change his approach to student leadership for the upcoming school year, never settling on anything that consistently worked from year to year. As Brad watched the students receive their diplomas, he chuckled aloud. He realized he didn't even know how to measure whether a student-leadership approach was actually working. From an outsider's perspective, the ministry looked to be going well, but Brad sensed he wasn't hitting on all cylinders quite yet. His student-leadership team seemed mechanical, without vibrancy. While his "A team" was good at running the programs of ministry, Brad had yet to solve the mystery of how to help his most spiritually grounded kids become natural at sharing their faith with their friends.

On that hot afternoon at the high school, Brad's reflective desires to effectively measure student leadership success took him from memories of past struggles to the images of what he would like to see as successful student ministry. The pictures didn't come easily. All Brad knew for certain was that his youth ministry seemed stuck and needed to move to a new level of vitality.

Chances are, Brad isn't the only youth worker sweating it out over how to help a group move to new depths in their experience of God. It's also likely that a lot of youth workers don't yet see a key number of their teenagers stepping up each year to help their friends make commitments to Christ. How could this not lead to a certain amount of frustration? We encounter desires, struggles, cycles, and emotions that often are mirrored in other youth workers around the country—a natural consequence when men and women pour themselves so unselfishly into the lives of students for the kingdom of God.

While all the youth ministries in our study were healthy by youth-ministry standards, they all had their own unique faith histories. It was part of the research strategy to listen to groups tell these stories.

Our team members were traveling home from one such visit and started one of the most memorable discussions of our two-year study. We concluded that—based on our observations—groups may actually reveal something of their spiritual vitality through such group interviews. Further, we theorized there actually might be different stages of spiritual vitality that groups move through, each predicting different degrees of evangelism effectiveness. For example, while some youth ministries did well at building unity, they didn't yet describe deeper experiences with God. Other ministries had an air of expectancy that God would use them to reach out to their schools, while some students expressed excitement over simply having a youth ministry at their church.

After a lot of discussion, the research team agreed that we had heard data reflecting four distinct stages of vitality. We also checked our discussion notes and assigned each of the groups to the stage of vitality we thought most accurately described them. Then we performed additional statistical analyses to see if the data we had collected through our surveys supported our hypothesis about these stages of vitality. The results were impressive enough that the implications are cause for reflection, especially among veteran youth workers who may be able to detect the various stages of vitality in their own ministry histories.

It isn't our intent to be critical of youth ministries, no matter what stage they may be in. Rather we want to describe what we found among some of the best youth ministries in the country, believing that youth workers can benefit from considering stages of development for their own groups. When groups lack an outreach orientation, displaying selfishness, they simply need to recognize that they must grow out of this stage of vitality into a greater level of collective maturity and faithfulness. These groups—not yet displaying fervor or effectiveness in evangelism—are nonetheless healthy because they are so well-positioned to continue their growth.

The Love-Flowing Stage

For each of the stages, we labored to come up with a description that fit the pattern of group interaction we observed. In the love-flowing stage, *a loving and caring atmosphere is established so that most group members and visitors affirm its presence.* Up and running at a "youth ministry as usual" pace, the borders of a youth ministry in this stage are clearly defined. That is, each member of the group knows who is and who isn't a part of the group. The conversations heard from members of this type of group centered around the organizational culture of the youth ministry—the youth pastor's tenure, the excitement surrounding a new program, or the anticipation of an upcoming event. Members prayed for others to become Christians when they gathered each week, but they seldom invited and hardly ever prayed for opportunities to share with others.

> In the love-flowing stage, a loving and caring atmosphere is established so that most group members and visitors affirm its presence.

It's not that these groups didn't believe evangelism was important, but they didn't act like they had a sense of outreach responsibility. Having said that, they did care for others in their group and worked hard to love each other faithfully.

The Peer-Encouragement Stage

In this stage, *peer ministry is so normal that students easily cite "one anothering" examples of how teenagers in the group help each other grow in their faith.*

This stage is significantly set apart from the love-flowing stage by the way students talk about their group. There are plenty of specific examples of how students ministered to one another. This type of group not only works at unity, but also shares notable experiences together, cares for one another in substantial ways, and easily recalls illustrations of each when given the opportunity. That's not all. They become a purposeful dependent community, cultivate a healthy image at school, and pray weekly for opportunities to share their faith in Christ.

> In this stage, peer ministry is so normal that students easily cite "one anothering" examples of how teenagers in the group help each other grow in their faith.

One distinctive feature of this stage is that students are involved in planning various events and meetings. They value their youth ministry and work hard to keep it warm, active, and fresh. "When I came into the group, it was easy to walk in because everyone was so friendly," one student leader told us.

The students in these groups still lived a faith life somewhat removed from their non-Christian friends and seldom prayed with others for opportunities to share their faith in Christ. Though there was a lot of peer encouragement, the focus we heard was on how others helped encourage *them*. They also talked about *their* role in the youth ministry: "I really like doing drama. It's my thing."

When asked to identify the most important factors contributing to the success of their ministry, students' responses included good role models, caring leaders, big groups, and good topics. One student added, "Prayer is important...but individual prayer." One small group echoed this, saying their youth ministry was successful because of "students' individual focus on God." Other student comments are also revealing. "It's important to be loving, not judging others." "Have students invite their friends to participate in youth activities."

Few in these groups have ever on their own, helped someone become a Christian. They've seen youth workers do it—sometimes quite often—but it's not something they think about on a regular basis. In fact, while it didn't come up in student discussions with us, youth workers made comments about how to foster evangelism. "We need to help our kids focus on one or two non-Christian friends who they can pray for and develop a strategy for sharing Christ with them."

It's likely that a vast number of youth ministries in America are in this stage. Though healthy ministry certainly can take place in this stage, there's still room to grow. One new girl understood the challenges ahead of her but appreciated her group's role in her life. "I try to reach out [like her group reached out to her] but it's scary. Our group's really laid-back and they accept *everybody*, because my closet is still quite full of stuff I need to deal with."

Big Gulf

Between the first two and the last two stages of vitality *is a big gulf, one that reveals perceptible differences in the language and evangelism activity of the groups.* We labeled this the big gulf for one reason: It *is* a big leap for a group. The ministry departs from the "youth ministry as usual" focus to move into a posture of dependence on God. They want to see him work in their lives as they minister beyond the natural borders of the group. Two significant characteristics are prominent on the healthier side of the big gulf. The first is a significant increase in prayer; the second is an indication that both the students and the adults have moved past their fears. They want to be increasingly selfless as they learn to be God-dependent.

Between the first two and the last two stages of vitality is a big gulf, one that reveals perceptible differences in the language and evangelism activity of the groups.

The God-at-Work Stage

In this stage, *an atmosphere of expectancy regarding the work of God is present such that students report as normal that God intervenes in their lives to powerfully answer prayer.*

In this stage, an atmosphere of expectancy regarding the work of God is present such that students report as normal that God intervenes in their lives to powerfully answer prayer.

During historical reflection, these groups talked about a God who is active and still interested in drawing people to himself. These groups showed clear evidence of their love for God and had seen him change lives. Their conversations about non-Christian friends revealed their understanding that God is still the loving Father at the end of the lane looking for his prodigal sons and daughters. One student shared, "You can't walk into our youth group without noticing God." It's this confident expectation that God is going to do something that changes the language and behavior of the group.

Students in these groups leave their houses every day with an awareness that God will be active in their lives. That makes it easy for them to pray, invite, and tell.

Three observable behaviors point to this expectancy of God at work. These groups aggressively initiate prayer, experience a tighter community of faith, and focus on improving their witnessing efforts.

Students who are part of groups at this stage of vitality don't wait for adults to structure their prayer times for them. They pray during the week for opportunities to share, pray with others more regularly, and make efforts to organize others for prayer. If we were to drop in on a meeting of such a group, we would likely see a few pockets of students off to the side praying before and after the gathering. If we followed these young people at school, we'd probably spot them in a classroom praying with their weekly student-led groups before the morning bell rings. For teenagers in this stage, prayer is not just important; it needs to become a public practice. It's integral to who they are and to their outreach to others. As one student shared, "We know that twelve men changed the world, so we know we can make an impact."

Prayer at this stage of vitality was clearly different from prayer in earlier stages. It no longer involved the individualized approach we observed in the peer-encouragement stage. This became clear when one student shared, "Prayer is big, both individual and corporate. Some meet every day for prayer during lunch at school. This is a close-knit community."

This expectancy that God will work also created a greater unity and commitment to honesty among group members. The groups truly cared about being the body of Christ (1 Corinthians 12:12-31) and talked frequently at a "most honest" level about the health of the body. One student reflected on the level of caring in her church group saying, "We invite and hug, but only when they're hurting." Another disclosed, "Although we have a really awesome atmosphere of love, I've talked to four kids who don't feel included."

The link between unity in a youth ministry and the understanding that God authors it was clear when one student said, "There's a lot of transparency among people at youth group. Lots of people there are *very real*. It's not just weird. It's God."

There was yet one more behavioral distinctive among groups at this stage of vitality. They organized efforts to go and verbally share the gospel with others. This may mean they set aside specific weeks for individuals to share their faith at meetings or committed special evenings as a team to go out and share their faith at a mall, on the street, or while calling on students at their homes. "I go out of my way to get to know students outside of Young Life," said one student. Another added, "I am motivated by God's command to spread the faith. Seeing God work through me keeps me going." One youth pastor clued us in to the fact that adult leaders were "keepers of the values" when he said, "It is absolutely essential that students be equipped and trained in evangelism and that they practice their on-the-job training weekly."

The Evangelism Expectancy Stage

This stage is *a subtle extension of the God-at-work stage, where the atmosphere of expectancy includes students anticipating that God will use them to reach others for Christ.* Groups in this stage of vitality not only love God and see his hand at work in their lives, but they come to expect that he will move through them to bring about evangelism fruit.

They expect success from their outreach efforts, not *due* to their efforts, but because they know God loves to be active in the work of those who follow him truly. So they work harder than do other groups on the priority of evangelism. Somehow these expectations of results combine with a strong evangelism value to bring about focused, increased outreach efforts.

> This stage is a subtle extension of the God-at-work stage, where the atmosphere of expectancy includes students anticipating that God will use them to reach others for Christ.

Three student behaviors set the groups at this stage apart from others. Students pray almost daily for opportunities to share their faith, they memorize God's Word significantly more often than their counterparts in other groups, and they reinvest themselves into formal ministries with a renewed focus on outreach.

Many of us would rejoice if our groups simply took the initiative to pray together weekly, as was descriptive of those in the peer-encouragement stage. Imagine what kind of

> This positive cycle simply spirals upward through the groups in this stage, creating a great sense of anticipation about not *if* but *when* the Lord will move to bring particular non-Christian friends into his kingdom.

real outreach focus would be owned among those students if the standard climbed to daily prayers with others that were targeted specifically toward evangelism. When we pray specifically, we see God answer prayers in specific ways. This positive cycle simply spirals upward through the groups in this stage, creating a great sense of anticipation about not *if* but *when* the Lord will move to bring particular non-Christian friends into his kingdom.

Their ambitious patterns of memorizing Scripture also feed this enthusiasm. God is *worthy* of such an investment, and he proves his love for us in new ways each time he acts in our lives. Obviously, disciplines of memorization also heighten the focus factor. God is at work; those who are attentive to God know that from their experience.

As students begin to taste the way God uses them to reach their friends, to touch them for eternity, they seem to become addicted to outreach. This is how we understood the patterns of students whose groups identified most with this particular stage of spiritual vitality. Impassioned as they were, they couldn't wait to tweak their programs in the direction of evangelism effectiveness. They wanted more!

Each of these three behaviors suggested a certain level of maturity; we saw the whole package in Alison. She invited friends often "because I want them to become Christians." She had confidence when she invited them because "everyone in my group is in tune with the gospel and wants to share it." She was on an evangelism team that went to a mall just two weeks prior to talking with us, and she had gone with a friend who had no experience in sharing the gospel. "I trained her by letting her watch me a few times, and I quizzed her as we walked. She hesitated to share her faith and was nervous, so I helped clarify."

It's a Good Start

It would be nice if we had a "quick" answer on how to get a group from one stage to another. We're not sure there is one. In fact, we want to stress that we sort of stumbled onto this "stages of vitality" business while conducting student-leadership research. More investigation on this theory is needed.

This much we know: Groups travel toward maturity on a difficult, bumpy path, and they need an informed commitment from leadership to make progress. Those in this project who gave us the privilege of scrutinizing them give us all hope that we can do better in seeing teenagers reach teenagers for Christ.

CHAPTER 8

Implications for Contemporary Youth-Ministry Models

Youth ministry collects workers under a variety of different tents. One of the first choices college grads wanting to head into the field must make is whether they want to work in a local church or a parachurch organization. That decision usually will impact the type of additional schooling needed, the sort of lifestyle one can expect, and the affiliations that will shape the career of the youth worker. The options are practically endless, as are the reasons people have for making their choices. Some decide to identify themselves with the kinds of ministries in which they grew up. Others choose on the basis of geography or family considerations. And many pick their professional niches because their own passion, gifts, and calling lead them into heartfelt partnership with people who are like them.

While it's not possible to profile every type of youth ministry, there are some major families we can describe. Within those families each youth worker—volunteer or paid— will make practical decisions about the role of student leadership within the ministry. How can our research be of practical help in these decisions?

The goal of this chapter is relatively straightforward. We want to "dialogue" with a number of the key youth-ministry models in practice today about the implications our student-leadership research may have for their approaches to ministry. We'll do our best to accurately represent the models of ministry we talk about, confessing that there is always a margin of error when observers are not "insiders" to a particular model. (The truth is, those who are insiders often bring their own blind spots to exercises of self-examination.) At any rate, because of this limitation we will be careful not to make overstatements. However, it's clear to us that the best use of this chapter will be to consider it a springboard for discussion by those who are already committed to the youth-ministry models being described.

Finally, this chapter—as much as any in this book—should be considered open to revision. Someone's particular youth-ministry philosophy may not be represented at all in these pages. New models have a way of popping up frequently in this innovative world of youth ministry. Our advice to readers who can't exactly locate their own brand of youth work in these next few pages is to take the following two steps. First identify the core commitments and distinctives of your approach to youth ministry. Then prayerfully reflect on the research presented in this book and ask the Lord to show you the one or two areas from the study that may help you improve your approach to student leadership.

That's been our approach to this chapter.

At-Risk-Youth Ministries

There are a number of specialized ministries who have targeted their work to narrow segments of the youth culture that, for a variety of reasons, are at-risk in their development. For example, some urban ministries focus on reaching out to gang members, recognizing that this social group is tremendously influential in the lives of thousands of young people. Ministries to teenage mothers have sprung up all over the country. Halfway houses and other short-term residential living approaches have been developed to help young people who are runaways, as well as those caught up in destructive addictions. Others have chosen to work with teenagers tangled in the legal system through court-referral programs or detention center chaplaincies. Though the nature of each of these specialized ministries makes it unfair to lump them all together, they face some common difficulties when it comes to implementing student leadership.

With the possible exception of gang-oriented ministries, each of the above approaches faces limitations that accompany the way youth workers even come into contact with these young people. It is crisis that brings them together, and much of the ministry strategy is to provide Christian intervention in the midst of crisis. Consequently, the most common form of youth ministry with at-risk kids may be characterized as short-term but intense.

With regard to student leadership, short-term ministry is a liability. It takes time to develop, or *disciple*, student leaders. The most explosive student leadership takes place when teenagers emerge as exemplary models of peer influence among other teenagers. And, as we'll discuss in the next chapter, there may be natural developmental limitations that simply keep us from starting the process of student leadership earlier than the teenage years.

On the other hand, ministry *intensity* could be a real asset when it comes to student leadership. Those familiar with short-term mission trips know it's possible to compress great spiritual growth into small time frames when there is intensity of focus. For example, it actually may be easier to help students in a residential living situation to pray together every day—even multiple times a day—for non-Christian friends.

The key to student leadership in these ministries is for adults to stay alert. When students experience a Christ-generated turnaround, they have brand-new potential! These young people often are responsive to intense adult involvement in their lives (at least weekly). They may, on occasion, step into the storm around them as living examples of hope to those still trapped in despair. The situations we're describing present too much instability to predict consistent student leadership effectiveness. But opportunistic youth workers wise in the ways of influence know that God sends student leaders everywhere to help pull off his ultimate rescue plan.

Community Centers

Another variation of youth ministry is built around a location where teenagers can drop in and enjoy some recreation or music. Sometimes these places also feature educational services like tutoring and computer access. Programmed activities try to pull in new students, and there are plenty of nonformal opportunities for just hanging out.

The challenge in applying student leadership to drop-in centers is to identify a consistent population of participating teenagers. If that group can be defined, there is no reason student leaders can't be developed from among them.

An attractive dimension of community centers is the casual feel for teenagers, unhurried and comfortable. This model usually avoids accusations that adults are too controlling in their work with teenagers. If teenagers think the facilities and programming are quality, there is a rich opportunity for student leaders to invite their friends into helpful surroundings as they seek to reach them for Christ. It is, of course, critical that student leaders have a high degree of ownership in the center. It must be *their* home.

And as is true for any inviting strategies, students should be trained how to best use the available adult-provided resources. For example, when student leaders know that at certain hours each week a particular pool-playing, fun-loving adult will be roaming the tables with a cue stick, they'll be alert to inviting the right friends for a game of eight ball. Of course, while racking 'em up, they can also be praying and looking for opportunities to use telling strategies.

Many times the adults involved in community centers invest themselves primarily in the facility upkeep. No small effort is needed for this important task. It's important that leaders also consider the encouragement the sharpest young people need from them. If student leaders will rise to their greatest potential, adults may need to meet weekly with them for accountability and support.

Denominational Affiliations

The only distinct model of youth ministry some people are committed to is that which is planned for them by their denominational leadership. Obviously, with the varieties in denominations, it's very difficult to address this as a "model" with regard to student leadership. Nonetheless, there is one feature that seems to be common among youth ministries that would identify themselves primarily by their denominational affiliation. The best students are usually trained in the ways of the denominational culture itself. They learn its history, get familiar with its organization, catch on to its worship styles, and discover its theological convictions. This is often done through camps, conventions, or curriculum.

When this happens, it provides a vision of student leadership that potentially competes with what has been developed in this book. Student leaders are asked to grow into becoming church leaders by those committed to this youth-ministry approach. They are to be ready to lead within their denominations with passion, experience, and education.

Our suggestions to those operating within this model do not include abandoning legitimate denominational agendas in order to bring about student-leader effectiveness. But they do include reviewing the primary purposes to which their youth ministries are committed. If evangelism is one of the top priorities in one's youth ministry, then denominational purposes will ultimately be best served when teenagers grow into effective agents of influence among their peers. They will be equipped for service in God's kingdom. They will only enrich their home churches when they return at later ages wanting to live as unselfishly as those models that nurtured them while they were growing up. Those who prize evangelism won't be sorry if they adjust their student-leadership strategies to incorporate the findings described in this book. There is plenty of room to "flavor" student-leadership strategies to denominational tastes. And their needs for denominational leadership certainly will be met by the God who promises to take care of our needs when we put God's kingdom first (Matthew 6:33).

Family-Based Youth Ministry

We have seen a range of approaches among those who identify with family-oriented youth ministries. At least four distinctions have been suggested to describe how families ought to be included in one's youth-ministry strategies (Dave Rahn, "Parafamily Youth Ministry," Group Magazine, May/June 1996). Some of these strategies more naturally fit the evangelism purposes of youth ministry than others.

In fact, the evangelism focus of student leadership is sometimes in tension with family-based youth-ministry models. This is largely because the reason for developing a youth-ministry model around family structures usually has more to do with the nurture/discipleship purposes of youth ministry than with outreach.

Are the two priorities incompatible? Not at all. In fact, it's hard to imagine a more exciting approach to ministry than having families, youth workers, and teenagers all on the same page, dedicated to helping student leaders become outstanding peer evangelists. We already know that most of the student leaders from our study reported that their parents were responsible for helping them come to faith in Christ. We also know that these same students seldom—if ever—see their parents engaged in evangelism activities. The clear challenge is to incorporate parents into meaningful roles as models, encouragers, and supportive resources in the development of their sons and daughters as student leaders.

When families get together around the common priority of outreach, P.I.T. (pray, invite, tell) strategies expand their potential incredibly. No one is in better position for frequent prayer partnering than a parent. Very few invitations are as attractive as those to hang out in a friendly, open home (especially if there's unlimited fridge access). And conversations on the couch or at the kitchen table have the advantage of natural sincerity, a convincing dimension to consider when telling others about Jesus.

Fellowship of Christian Athletes

In thousands of high schools around the country, Christian coaches and teachers sponsor "huddles" of Christian students that help kids take strong and meaningful stands as Christians in their schools. While the ministry does not seek to exclude non-athletes, it's clear that their longtime strategy has centered around helping athletes—historically among the most influential students in their schools—assert themselves as Christian leaders among their peers.

Adult volunteers play the key role in establishing FCA groups at particular schools. There are a huge number of huddles across the country, and a lot of differences between them. Some are all about helping Christian kids connect with each other in meaningful ways. If evangelism happens, it's almost accidental. Others work hard toward the vision of reaching beyond themselves to share their faith with others. Some have a tremendously popular image in their schools and others are nearly invisible.

Why the big differences? The most satisfactory explanation may be the variation between local adult leaders. It's no surprise that FCA's camp and retreat ministries are so well-received. With pooled resources and the support of professional staff, those activities can establish a dependable level of quality. How can the same sort of quality be standardized across the vast network of ministries following this model? Maybe our findings on adult roles could be adopted as a common basis for the job description of huddle leaders everywhere. We think providing quality resources, inspirational models, and weekly coaching is a three-part job description FCA's adults could naturally understand and implement.

We'd like to offer one additional caution, one that is probably unnecessary for the majority of those who identify with this ministry model. Student leadership as defined in this book is not automatically aligned with particular interest groups like athletes. In fact, our research did not reveal a high correlation between students who are considered socially popular and those who are effective in peer outreach. Generally, student leaders are difficult enough to discover and develop. If they must also be athletes, the job is much tougher.

First Priority

A fairly recent development among youth-ministry models, First Priority uses a strategy built on the assumption that students can minister to their friends more effectively than any adults. Adult youth workers in a community participate together to support students as they establish campus-based Christian ministries.

It's hard to disagree much with the strategies of First Priority when you're writing a book describing the potential of student leadership. Certainly the idea that teenagers are capable of taking both initiative and responsibility for reaching out to their friends is in harmony with our vision of student leadership. Our only concerns have to do with what adults should do while student ministry takes place. While we acknowledge that adults may often need to "get out of the way" in order to help students develop as leaders, our research clearly identifies key and active roles for adults who bring out the best in student-leader evangelism effectiveness. When—or if—the First Priority model undervalues the importance of these adult contributions, we are fearful that tempting shortcuts today could have negative long-term consequences. We'd be thrilled if cooperating youth workers leading First Priority strategies in a community resolved to adopt a high standard: Spiritually mature adults will somehow be connected to all student leaders weekly.

Can you tell we believe adult roles in youth ministry should not be minimized? We'd like to follow up with an additional observation. Wherever student-leadership models tip toward encouraging teenagers to take over and shape ministries as they see fit—a possibility when adults are not available as resources—it's likely that students will invest themselves heavily in programming. When teenagers spend their energy in this way, evangelism outcomes are diminished, not strengthened. Our prediction—based on insights derived from our study—is that such approaches may have first-generation effectiveness as measured against the goal of student evangelism. But the energy diverted from pray, invite, and tell strategies will eventually take its toll with the result being a Christian campus club that is relatively ineffective in outreach. Let the adult leaders committed to the First Priority model stay vigilant as they monitor the effectiveness of this exciting new ministry.

Purpose-Driven™ Youth Ministry

Youth workers who identify with Doug Fields' helpful book will recognize how friendly *Purpose-Driven™ Youth Ministry* is to student-leadership purposes. Youth ministries, as subsets of churches, are urged to discover the five biblical purposes of ministry. One of these nonnegotiable purposes—evangelism—is largely brought about when students are discipled so they can do ministry. Those students who move through the ministry's process of spiritual growth, who most typify the important values of the youth ministry, are core students who may become student leaders. We love high expectations.

Purpose-Driven™ Youth Ministry's declaration about the importance of adult models couldn't be stronger. Similarly, when student leaders are asked to take the friendship-evangelism challenge, they are being called to model peer evangelism among the other teenagers in their group. If those who are committed to this well-developed philosophy of youth ministry are not seeing people become Christians as a result of peer-to-peer outreach, we suggest they pay close attention to whether or not students are actually living P.I.T. strategies in front of their friends. When we know we have a solid strategy, we want to make sure we have the right people implementing the strategy.

As a final suggestion, we note that the most committed students are periodically asked to develop the profile of a student leader's role. This is a great idea, helping those who must live by the standards to truly own them. It may be that as students consider the research presented here, they could adopt P.I.T. as a performance expectation by which to judge their own modeling effectiveness. That may be a practical way for one nonnegotiable ministry purpose (evangelism) to be established in student leaders' lives.

"Skyscraper" Approaches

Given the understanding that leadership is inherently connected to influence, it's not surprising that some in youth ministry suggest that every Christian ought to be considered a leader-in-training. The term "skyscraper" is meant to describe the picture of leadership development that compresses the base of the more common "pyramid" model. It depicts a ministry approach where all participants are developed to be student leaders. Chances are, those approaching youth ministry with this mindset look through our study in order to implement the strategies among *all* the young people in their ministries—if not immediately, at least eventually.

We don't want to discourage this lofty ambition. In truth, there is no reason youth workers cannot plan for such 100 percent participation at the leadership level. Given the recommendations from our study, this optimistic preparation would include recruiting enough spiritually mature adults to play the role of active mentor-coaches in teenagers' lives. Remember that adults who meet at least weekly with their younger brothers and sisters make the greatest difference in their lives; this high standard should be kept in mind during recruitment.

Extra organizational effort might also be needed for those youth workers wanting to creatively facilitate prayer efforts among their group. It will also be important to ensure that all students have access to quality feedback so they can help improve the meetings and events they want to invite their friends to. Sometimes training students to tell others about Jesus is best served by hands-on experiences, where larger groups require considerably more resources.

> The reality is that while there is nothing wrong with planning for high levels of involvement, not every student is ready to actually apply the challenges of praying, inviting, and telling.

The reality is that while there is nothing wrong with planning for high levels of involvement, not every student is ready to actually apply the challenges of praying, inviting, and telling. Not all will commit to weekly meetings with adults. When it becomes clear that they don't all show up at large-group outreach meetings, it's likely they'll also avoid more serious training events.

When students don't measure up to leadership expectations, their youth workers are faced with basically two choices, even as they continue to encourage the best from their teenagers. They can adjust their expectations (and organizational structures!) to accommodate the reality that not everyone is ready to grow at the same pace (this is our recommendation). Or they can dilute the meaning of student leadership, running the risk of discouraging those who are eager to respond to every challenge of spiritual growth.

Sonlife

The philosophy of ministry taught by Sonlife and adopted by hundreds of youth workers around the world is appealing to many, largely because it's derived from Jesus' ministry strategy. One of the additional principles trumpeted is that disciple-making strategies ought to be bent to whatever growth level is appropriate for students. We couldn't agree more. This leads naturally to the conclusion that certain kids, when they "pop up" and display faithfulness and motivation to follow Jesus closer, need to be trained to minister to others. Taken in the natural course of events, this usually begins as students look for ways to serve humbly. From that point many will grow to serve their friends by sharing their faith with them.

There is nothing in this model that's in conflict with our student-leadership research. Outreach events that meet quality standards are coached as excellent strategies, easing the task of student leaders who want to tell their invited friends about Jesus. However, we want to stress that these programmed events do not instill the value of evangelism nearly as well as those youth workers and students who themselves are modeling evangelism. For men and women who personally are passionate about evangelism, Sonlife's philosophy will naturally and deliberately improve ministry-team efforts by incorporating the student-leadership research findings presented here.

Student-Led Cell Groups

Cell groups have been a crucial form of ministry effectiveness for as long as the church has existed. More recently, models of youth ministry have been developed around the nearly exclusive use of this method. Flexibility, close relationships, and rapid multiplication are all great reasons to use small groups. In this particular model of youth ministry, adults also play a wonderfully encouraging role, very much consistent with the standards discovered in our research.

We have tried to make the case that if students are to be involved in leading programs as part of their student-leadership responsibilities, adult leaders must take care that students don't get swamped with organizational details. Leading a small group—buoyed by the supportive resources of an adult—is an assignment that nicely sidesteps most of those concerns. There is much to be commended in this model as it relates to student-leader effectiveness.

Our only suggestion is one that expands the model in dramatic, perhaps unacceptable ways. The research showed that the resource used most often by student leaders when they wanted to invite their friends to a setting where evangelism could be helped along was large-group meetings. And the most effective of our peer evangelists used this inviting strategy frequently. Given this observation, it seems a shame not to include some sort of large-group experience as part of a youth ministry's overall evangelism strategy.

Willow Creek Student Impact

It's not surprising that the youth-ministry model that has evolved from a church built for evangelism effectiveness includes a student-leadership component that is fairly consistent with the findings of our research project. Close examination of Bo Boshers' work reveals an important discovery. While evangelism fruit drives the vision of student ministry, leadership development is the overriding strategy.

Two organizational constants communicate Student Impact's values. Because a teenager's natural point of contact—and influence—is based in his or her high-school community, each student is identified with the campus team from that person's school. Message 1: "We're committed to providing you with the quality programming connections that will help you reach your peers." In addition, everyone who is involved in student ministry comes under the care of a leader who focuses on no more than five people. Message 2: "We're committed to helping you truly develop your potential in Christ." The first message fits the evangelism vision of student leadership we wrote about in chapter 1. The second rings true with the disciple-making focus necessary to develop student leaders (chapter 2).

The best contribution this research may make for those who've adopted the student-impact model is to reinforce much of their strategy while detailing standards of effectiveness for student leaders.

Young Life

As one of the pioneers in youth evangelism, Young Life has developed core values that have served the kingdom of God well over the years. They've adopted their founder's conviction that it's a sin to bore a kid, and that translates into a commitment to quality programs and caring relationships as the vehicles in which the gospel message will be carried. No one does evangelism camps better or is more committed to quality throughout those camping experiences. Adult staff—paid and volunteer—see themselves primarily as missionaries to teenagers. As a result, the idea of student leadership as described in this book should not be widely practiced in Young Life circles.

But is it? While not formally identified as student leaders, kids who've become Christians are encouraged to become part of Campaigners, small discipleship groups led by mature adults committed to relational ministry at all levels. This structure nicely fits the role of adults described in this book. And what student-leader type wouldn't love to have quality resources like Young Life meetings, camps, and caring adults to which they can invite their friends? If P.I.T. strategies were woven throughout the Campaigner curriculum, there is no reason that student leaders, clandestine though they may be in the Young Life model, could not become very effective.

In fact, we'd like to disclose a little secret. One of the most effective student-leader sites visited in our research study was a Young Life group tinkering with the potential that peer evangelism could have in their ministry. To which we say: Go for it!

Youth Churches

More common in Europe than in the United States, youth churches have been developed by those whose mentality parallels that of church planters. Like those who start such mission work, there is a willingness to accept short-term limitations to a church's full profile of maturity in order to launch a truly effective work in evangelism. There is also an interest in paying sharp attention to the needs, interests, and wants of the group being targeted for outreach. That's why youth churches have been started—to reach youth.

In their truest form, youth dominate the programming leadership. They lead music, teach, shepherd, and organize. Because of their high levels of involvement, there is no question that the church can be at least friendly to the youth culture.

Obviously this role by students is highly demanding, so much that those invested with the most organizational responsibilities would be best to lower their expectations with regard to their personal evangelism fruitfulness. They should come to see themselves as the adults in our study, whose duties included providing quality resources that would help communicate the gospel. By doing so, they will help other youth members of the church (those less invested "up front") to communicate their Christian faith effectively. In addition, P.I.T. strategies have the simplicity and focus to be genuinely valuable to a youthful congregation.

We can't advocate the withdrawal of adults entirely from the mix of this youth min-istry. But it's OK if adults confine themselves to the low-profile small-group life coaching described in chapter 3. This will help ensure that passing on the faith (as Paul described in 2 Timothy 2:2) will be an act of faithfulness rather than inventiveness.

Youth for Christ

When YFC trains their new staff to do ministry, they teach nine nonnegotiable stan-dards of practice they want everyone to pursue with diligence and balance. One of those standards is student leadership. It should follow that the findings of this study will be well-received by these parachurch evangelists. In fact, we were troubled that there weren't more nominations from YFC ranks that could have been investigated as a part of our research.

Chapter 2 contains an admonition well-suited for those who engage in evangelism with an urgency mindset. If we let the immediate demands of non-Christian kids drive our strategies, we may sacrifice both quality and people development. The reason is simple: Both require a great amount of time.

Within YFC, Campus Life serves as the main high school model, and student leadership is one of the primary "relational ministry actions" staff are trained to implement. Since staff are viewed as missionaries to a particular school or community, often the focus of student leadership is heavy on inviting. Student leaders are encouraged to bring their non-Christian friends to a meeting so the adults can present the gospel. Giving more consideration to student-telling strategies and weekly adult coaching could only strengthen Campus Life.

YFC's structure is wonderfully poised to employ the findings of this research to improve evangelism through student leadership. Their DC/LA Conferences are exceptional events, de-signed to stir Christian students toward personal evangelism. They care deeply about non-Christian kids. If they focus on the faithful processes of development, strategically commit-ting themselves to the roles and disciplines key adults must assume, they will see increased evangelism fruit through student leaders, and God's church will be healthier.

Youth Groups

As we surveyed the variety of youth-ministry models in practice today, we were en-couraged that so many youth ministries have a clear sense of direction. But we also believe a number of churches have not done the work of choosing their philosophies intentionally.

By default, they meet together weekly without much purpose or focus. They do activities and can likely identify leaders within their groups. After all, leaders always emerge, don't they? For purposes of addressing those trapped in such a cycle of ineffectiveness, we've chosen to label these "youth groups." Obviously, not every ministry calling itself a youth group deserves the critique we're supplying here.

But our concern cannot be overstated. Without a clear purpose or strategy, these groups will move in whatever direction their "student leaders" lead. And chances are, these influencers won't lead in the direction of a ministry of evangelism. They aren't the student leaders described in this book and won't become so until adult leaders shape their youth ministries in purposeful ways, committed to discipleship that results in evangelism.

Youth Worship Teams

Increasing numbers of churches—and youth ministries—are discovering the sheer joy and attractiveness of worship together. As a result, whole youth ministries are formulated around the experience of worshipping God. Earnest singing and prayer, coupled with high-quality music bands and impressive technology, do have a winsome quality that many groups are finding to be effective.

We can't deny that worship is one of the purposes of the church. It's certainly a legitimate expression of student leadership, and it was a prominent feature in most of the youth ministries in our research. Our concern is that when worship teams are not counterbalanced with intentional evangelism efforts, they can lead to youth ministries that love being together and neglect reaching out.

The focus of this book is on a particular role of student leadership: evangelism faithfulness. Another book and study may be necessary to explore the legitimate need student leaders have to be faithful in worship. Neither is acceptable alone. Those God has gifted and impassioned to lead others in worship should do so. And they must find ways to fight through the busyness of those demands so they can also pray for lost friends, invite them to potentially rich outreach situations, and tell them about Jesus. Adults who coach them in weekly mentoring relationships can help them balance the all-of-life call to faithfulness.

Chances are pretty good that we either missed a youth-ministry model or didn't catch the nuances of each model as accurately as we would have liked. But taken together, this interaction with some of the most common approaches to youth ministry on the contemporary scene should serve to reinforce the potential of student leadership anywhere.

CHAPTER 9:
Leadership and Issues of Adolescent Development

One of the great hopes we have for our findings on student leadership is that youth ministry will collectively take a giant step forward in both faithfulness and effectiveness. It's been easy to daydream about the influence of the research in this book. Even now we can imagine youth workers scribbling furiously as they lay out their plans and ministry strategies. (We'll share how this research has impacted our lives later.) Among the practical questions veterans of student leadership have learned to consider is whether there needs to be any age restrictions placed on those who will assume roles of leadership among their peers. In this chapter we will explore some related social-science research that may help us make this difficult decision in light of the best information available.

Jim is an example of the type of student who confounds us with regard to these screening decisions. As a high-school freshman he was eager, intent to learn, and wide-eyed in his enthusiasm. He had a contagious personality that dripped with natural charisma. Because he often laughed at himself without hint of cockiness, students who were older than Jim not only enjoyed him—they seemed to be carried along by the attractive sincerity of his Christian life. Before you make the decision as to whether or not you would choose to include Jim in your student leadership team, be assured that there were no skeletons in his youthful closet. We won't reveal some hideous, hidden character flaw that would allow us to easily reject Jim as a student leader "if we had only known." In Jim's case, everything about him as a high-school freshman was authentic, including his walk with the Lord Jesus.

Would you include him or exclude him from your student-leadership team? Some of you are puzzled that there is any debate at all in this decision. "What's to exclude?" you may be asking. And in this true anecdote, the only caution we offer at all is to wonder whether younger adolescents are *developmentally ready* for the responsibilities of peer leadership.

Before we ask you to lock in your vote for or against the inclusion of Jim on your student-leader team, take a moment to reflect on whatever history you've had in youth ministry. Can you identify times when you've had a large pool of enthusiastic freshmen enter your ministry, ready to do whatever was necessary in order to follow the Lord faithfully? Did they maintain or expand that level of dedication? Chances are, some did excel, but a significant number of others got bogged down in the cynical cycles of high-school existence too common across our country. The veteran youth workers we know sigh deeply as they recall how the ever-present twinkle in the eyes of too many teenagers gets replaced by the glazed and wary look of young adults educated by the harshness of their experiences. When the youthful idealism of sinful teenagers meets the reality of consequences, disappointments, and limitations, hope is wounded and optimism is a casualty. This is life, and adolescence often provides an introductory course that serves as a wake-up call for dreamers.

Jim hit this wall, and it rocked him so much that he never regained the confident influential stride he'd had. It's tough to isolate the causes for his fall from leadership ranks. Maybe it was the persistent cruelty of classmates who were determined to build themselves up by tearing him down. Perhaps it was the relentless and increased pressures he put on himself to achieve. Certainly being turned down by girls as he made his first trips into the world of teenage dating didn't help. Neither did seeing his heroes fail. When a neighbor boy died, Jim was hounded by a constant cloud of uncertainty. And how much influence should we attach to his first significant romantic relationship, which included sexual exploration and ended in disappointment and pain?

Some may protest that Jim's experience can't be described as normal for everyone. We agree. There are teenagers who have it much tougher and others who seem to catch a break from life. To be sure, many of our difficulties come from our own choices. But many do not, and the reality that life is unpredictably hard is so important to our human journey that we must do everything we can to equip young people with the hope and faith in Jesus Christ they need. How will they learn this great lesson about life's difficulties? Only experience can be counted on to deliver this message, and it is such a dispassionate tutor that we'd better be strategically positioned to support them as they plunge into their course of study.

> When the youthful idealism of sinful teenagers meets the reality of consequences, disappointments, and limitations, hope is wounded and optimism is a casualty. This is life, and adolescence often provides an introductory course that serves as a wake-up call for dreamers.

That's why some may hesitate to include freshmen (or younger youth) on their student-leadership teams. There's no real substitute for testing someone's faith through the fire of tough experiences before they land on a pedestal of leadership expectations.

What are the pressure points of development, the places that might produce cracks in faith's foundation when life's inevitable storms come? We can think of at least three areas worth keeping an eye on as our young people lean into life: identity development, social development, and moral development. Because identity issues are so huge, we'll give this concern the most consideration in the pages that follow. But each has implications for how effective student leaders can be as they seek to influence their friends for Jesus Christ.

Identity Development and Student Leadership

One of the great tasks we all negotiate as we grow up is to establish our self-identity. Teenagers need to learn who they are in relation to their friends and family. What values and convictions will they develop, from which their life's decisions will flow? Which activities will aid or hinder this public identity pursuit? With which groups will they affiliate? Further, which ones would they say best explain who they are?

It's as if each of us sometime during our development is handed a blank sheet of cosmic paper, one that eventually we are to use as we create the self-portrait we'll have to live with. There are some limitations in the drawing instruments available for our use; we can't make every choice related to our own identity formation. For example, we can't choose our biological families or the genetic codes that have endowed us with particular bodies, intelligence capabilities, or personalities. So given these tools, what will teenagers create? Who will they become? From what palette will they choose to paint?

James Marcia expanded upon Erik Erikson's work to help us understand something of the process of identity formation. His research led him to conclude that adolescents must experience a sense of *crisis* before they make the *commitment* necessary for identity achievement. The nature of this crisis period varies considerably between individuals. Some teenagers may spend years in this state of bewilderment, suspending their identity commitment until they have settled key questions. Others move through some periods of questioning without slowing down much at all. Marcia suggests that anyone who wants to be successful in negotiating the key issues about his or her own sense of identity must go through this moratorium time. It's as if young people are in an identity holding pattern before they can land their "self planes" safely (Rolf E. Muuss, *Theories of Adolescence*).

But Marcia's contributions also describe those who hit an important snag in their identity development. He uses the term "foreclosure" to identify young people who make their identity commitment before experiencing the crisis that brings true ownership. This comes from really wrestling with questions and issues so choices genuinely become their own. Sometimes they simply want to please their family members or church, and so their self-defining choices are, in a sense, corrupted. But these decisions aren't truly owned as *their* identity because they "closed the deal" prematurely.

If experience-based exploration and crises are important to the task of identity formation, how should we understand younger adolescents who signal that they are ready to become student leaders? There's a chance they may be confident that they have arrived, unaware that they have a lot of climbing ahead of them. If we suspect this is the case, we will be smart if we create some sort of student-leadership farm system, a place where teenagers can "try on" the commitments of student leadership that will help them in their necessary exploration.

We also don't want to rule out the possibility that some students really have been attentive to the identity options around them, truly have wrestled with soul-searching questions, and are genuinely ready to commit to following Jesus closely and influencing friends deeply. When we are satisfied that young people fit this profile, it's time to rejoice. We've got new ministry partners!

A page out of Jesus' coaching notes could really help us. He often invited casual followers to take a closer look. His parables rewarded those who were honestly hungry to apply his truth, separating them from the semi-passive crowd of note-takers. When he chose the Twelve, he knew they'd had enough experience with him that they could make informed choices to follow him in faith (Bruce Manning Metzger, *The New Testament: Its Background, Growth, and Content).* Their period of investigation (crisis?) had helped them know that they were ready to make the commitment (identity achievement?) of becoming his disciples. And Jesus respected the importance of this developmental need well enough that he constantly cautioned crowds against making popular, but premature, decisions to follow him.

We shouldn't be surprised that Jesus was so developmentally savvy. He was, after all, a participating partner in designing our identity-formation process.

Social Development and Student Leadership

David Elkind's concept of the "imaginary audience" is a powerful way to describe how teenagers' development may affect their relationships (David Elkind, *All Grown Up &*

No Place to Go). Young people move through their day convinced that their peers are always watching—no, *scrutinizing*—them. This adolescent egocentrism has a natural consequence for their relationships. How could a perspective that essentially reorders the world so that everything revolves around a person *not* have a considerable impact? More specifically, great numbers of teenagers live daily with a kind of terror that their watching peers will discover flaws that will possibly make them social lepers.

While this phenomenon is reportedly in place for all ages of adolescence, research shows that eighth graders are significantly more self-conscious than older adolescents. In fact, the older teenagers get, the less important it is to them that "everyone is watching" (Rolf E. Muuss, *Theories of Adolescence*).

But wait. There's more that suggests younger teenagers may be at a socially developed disadvantage when it comes to assuming roles of student leadership. Additional research indicates that middle adolescents (fourteen to sixteen years old) are at the peak of their susceptibility to the influence of friends. Before that age, parental influence is often stronger than that of friends. After that age, students demonstrate more of the self-confidence that comes from the identity achievement described earlier (Julia A. Graber et al., eds., *Transitions Through Adolescence: Interpersonal Domains and Context*).

Taken together, this research affirms some cautions we need to think about with regard to younger teenagers. Some may simply *care* too much about what friends think, making them more likely to try to please peers as they consider important choices affecting their Christian standards. We should be cautious when we decide which young teenagers are ready for student-leadership responsibility. But along the way we can also be confident that the influence of solid, older Christian teenagers may profoundly affect their younger friends.

Moral Development and Student Leadership

We can talk about at least two concerns when we try to understand what it means to grow in the moral domain of life. The first has to do with decision-making and the second with behavior. In both these areas, research helps us think about how teenagers may be growing. We'd like to focus on what may help us in our student-leadership strategies.

The research in moral decision-making has been dominated by the work of Harvard psychologist Lawrence Kohlberg. His contributions try to evaluate decisions without making judgments about whether a choice is right or wrong. Instead, they are assessed by the quality of the thinking that went into the decision. For that reason, Kohlberg would say the best moral decisions are not possible unless we are capable of the most thorough kind of analysis. Good thinking is necessary before we can make good decisions, moral or otherwise (Rolf E. Muuss, *Theories of Adolescence*).

Guess what? Young adolescents are just getting acquainted with their new brain packages. Their capacity to think about hypothetical situations and possibilities is a relatively new development for them. That means—according to Kohlberg—that they are limited in their moral decision-making processes because they are limited in their thinking. More specifically, they will typically decide that something is right or wrong on the basis of consequences ("it's only wrong if I get caught") or rules ("it's wrong if everybody says it's wrong") rather than principles ("it's wrong because it violates true ethical standards").

It may be that this limitation on the way kids make moral judgments should be important in choosing student leaders. If so, it will lead us to be cautious again when thinking about the youngest teenagers.

But these issues do not have to be what matters most to Christians when they think about moral growth. Kohlberg's work deals exclusively with *how* people think about matters of right and wrong; we are at least as concerned with *what* they think. We want kids to make the right moral choices and point to the Bible as the standard to guide them. In fact, there is evidence to suggest that post-adolescent Christians make moral decisions after filtering them through their most important commitment—their faith in Jesus Christ.

If kids make the right choices because they are Christians, they may be in a good position to influence their friends for the Lord. That assumes, of course, they actually live by their decisions. Actions speak louder than words. It's a disturbing reality that too often moral thinking does not necessarily lead to moral behavior. But what can we predict about moral *commitments*? A recent research study by Link Institute offers a mixed review:

• About 64 percent of a sample of Midwestern students who made public commitments to sexual abstinence in 1994 and 1995 reported that they were still living by that commitment in 1999, but only 52 percent of high-school students in our country are still virgins (Julia A. Graber et al., eds., *Transitions Through Adolescence: Interpersonal Domains and Context*). Is the difference worth celebrating?

• We identified 84 percent of those who made such a pledge in 1998 and could still say they had not yet had sex in 1999. Is that a good retention rate on such a commitment, only a year old?

• At least 56 percent and maybe 72 percent (ages were reported in spans of two years) of those making pledges in our study were fourteen years old or younger when they did so. This is in the face of a national standard reporting that 51 percent of sexually active students experienced their first intercourse before they were fourteen years of age (Julia A. Graber et al., eds., *Transitions Through Adolescence: Interpersonal Domains and Context*). Do they know what they're committing to?

Such statistics practically beg us to try to help teenagers make important moral decisions as early as we can. But as we can see, the reality is that there will be some slippage in their commitments, due in part to the fact that developmental changes are at "warp speed" in young adolescents.

Given some of the social-science insights presented in this chapter, how will you vote on the issue of putting young teenagers to work as student leaders? Our suggestion is to make sure the investment you make in these willing but youthful students is solid and thoughtful, but that you wait a while before heavily depending on them. By the time they're juniors they—and you—will have a much more stable picture of the kind of people they really want to become and the kind of student leaders they were created to be!

CHAPTER 10:
Putting It All Together

Hopefully as you've read this book God has challenged you with new horizons in student leadership. Whether you're a college student considering youth ministry or a veteran youth worker, it's important to consider the practical implications of potentially revolutionary ministry ideas. This chapter seeks to match our major themes with concrete steps to help along your student-leadership journey. We hope it's valuable as you try to develop mature and faithful student leaders, committed to reaching others for Jesus Christ.

The Leader Who Leads Them

We need to begin in our own back yard. If effective youth ministry in general is built on relationships, student leadership is more so. The closeness and frequent contact that dynamic and faithful student leadership requires means the youth leader and his or her life and values will be imparted to the students. We will transmit both the good and bad of who we are. This is the reality of modeling. As we noted before, it didn't take many research visits before the team of Huntington College students noticed that most student-leadership groups reflected the personalities of the youth leaders in action and speech.

As leaders, if our walk with Christ doesn't include a focus on prayer and evidence of our desire to share our faith with our peers, there's a good chance students won't develop a desire to pray and share their faith with their friends. The students in our ministry will most likely follow our example no matter what we're verbally teaching. When asked to share about their ministry success, the youth leaders in this research project were unanimous in their advice: *Youth leaders set the pace for their youth ministries.*

Who Should Be a Student Leader?

This may be one of the more controversial aspects of student leadership, singling out students from a youth ministry who'll move to an "inner circle" core group. Should you hand-pick your team, or do you give everyone a chance to be in student leadership? How important are relational skills, developmental concerns, particular talents, or learning qualities when making your decisions? While you obviously will be drawn to those natural leaders with engaging personalities, do you worry that there might be a "King David" (1 Samuel 16) out there who might be overlooked unless you select him or her for student leadership? Essentially these questions narrow to "What criteria will you use to choose students for your student-leadership team?"

> The potential problem of pride (serving for status) is replaced with purpose (serving others) as a student leader.

These questions can create many types of tension. Since we're advocating a form of student leadership that is akin to a New Testament approach, that of ministry and mission, some of these tensions will be eased. The potential problem of pride (serving for status) is replaced with purpose (serving others) as a student leader. When an evangelism focus for student leadership is emphasized, the vision crystallizes and the selection process eases as students who respond to that vision and focus emerge naturally.

There are three main phases to forming a student-leader team: selection, screening, and steppingstones. As we examine some criteria, perhaps we'll see that even the yet-to-be-king David would have made an excellent student leader at the shepherd boy's local high school.

Selection

The first step in the selection process should be no surprise—*pray diligently about what God wants you to do.* When we push away from the "shore" of a program-driven approach to ministry, we become dependent on the "wind" of the Holy Spirit to guide us as we lead. We must connect with the source of the wind in ministry and God's kingdom before moving out and inviting others to come with us on that journey. It's easy to fall into the trap of letting student leadership become another program if the Holy Spirit doesn't lead us. We'll lose the richness of a Christ-centered, people-focused approach if we are building *our* kingdom. It's God's. Give it to God and listen for God's voice guiding you how to proceed.

Next, *state in writing your expectations.* What is it that the student leaders will do? Write it down. What do you sense God wants you to do? Write that down. Will they meet weekly? two times a month? Will there be expectations of a devotional life? accountability? What is their job description? Spell it out as clearly as possible. Draw upon the findings reported in this book to support your expectations among adults and teenagers. Be sure other adults have a chance to participate with you in your formulations.

Some groups have taken on the praying, inviting, telling (P.I.T.) focus by giving themselves names like "The P.I.T. Crew" or "The P.I.T. Bulls." (The "Arm P.I.T.s" probably wouldn't be appropriate.) During the fall of 1999, Fellowship of Christian Athletes launched a challenge to students through their Internet home page to join the P.I.T. Crew. They used the Web and e-mail to collect and monitor student efforts in praying, inviting, and telling.

On the following page is a sample student-leader application from a youth ministry that uses the Student Leader Three-Step.

Student Leader Application

Requirements for a Student Leader

1. Calling: You can state confidently that you desire to be on the P.I.T. Crew because you feel God is calling you and you are burdened to see others come to Christ and grow in their faith.

2. Discipleship to Christ: You commit to maintain a close and faithful walk with Jesus Christ, evidenced by consistent devotions including Bible study, obedience to God's Word, prayer, the fruits of the Holy Spirit evident in your life, and times of reflective thinking. You are willing to be held accountable to this commitment by an adult staff member.

3. Consistent attendance: We will meet as a P.I.T. Crew two times a month on Sunday nights. Due to the importance of meeting together, you are allowed no unexcused absences from these meetings. If you miss a meeting and it is unexcused (meaning we don't know why you're missing), you'll be asked to meet with an adult staff member to discuss your absence.

4. Others-focused: Your participation in P.I.T. Crew is about God working through you to minister to others. Self-centeredness, chronic complaining, and lack of love for others are not part of P.I.T. Crew. This is a *service* group that will be focused on allowing God to use us to minister to and serve others. We will agree to hold each other accountable to this throughout the year.

5. Praying: We won't leave home (or church) without it! Our time with God, individually and corporately, is foundational to anything we do. If you are a P.I.T. Crew member, it is expected that you will be praying every day for the youth ministry and for your own evangelism efforts. We will pray with others regularly each month for opportunities to share our faith in Christ with our friends.

6. Inviting: This youth ministry is designed with an understanding that non-Christians will be attending regularly and at specific outreach events. We, as a P.I.T. Crew, will lead the charge in inviting others. No one outside the P.I.T. Crew should be out-inviting us!

7. Telling: If people outside P.I.T. Crew are asked to describe us, their first comment should revolve around our consistent example of what it means to be "Christian." Their second remark might center on verbal evangelism. We want to move past our fears and learn how to be effective in communicating God's love to others through word and action. We will help you get there, but the risk to share is obviously yours. If you're willing to *go for it,* then we're willing to help you get there.

8. Maturity: P.I.T. Crew is focused on ministry to others. This requires some maturity and ability to see the "big picture" clearly. As stated earlier, P.I.T. Crew is not another group to join for your own benefit, but it's a group focusing on reaching others with the love of Jesus Christ.

Commitment

If you have prayed about it, can answer honestly that you feel God is calling you to this, are willing to be pushed in your commitment to the expectations above, and would like to talk more about how to *go for it* on the P.I.T. Crew, then sign below and turn it in or mail it to the church office.

I have prayed about this and feel like God has given me permission to interview for P.I.T. Crew. I am willing to commit and be held accountable to the above expectations. I know that signing this does not guarantee that I am on the P.I.T. Crew. Please contact me to set up an interview.

Signed _____

Phone _____

Date _____

Screening

We mentioned it briefly in the previous chapter—a sifting process is required as students line up to be student leaders. It's important not to just take all applicants without first hearing their stories. We also need to clearly talk through the student-leadership vision and expectations.

Imagine that Evelyn wanted to be on your student-leadership team. Her folks held leadership positions in church, but Evelyn was shy and self-centered—she wasn't even very helpful at youth events. She couldn't bring herself to say that she felt like God was leading her to be a student leader. Could she blossom into a student leader with nurture and maturity? Sure. Was she ready to assume a role full of expectations like those spelled out above? No. Yet some would (we've done it before!) press ahead and put her on the team, hoping she'd grow into an effective peer minister but would be reaping poor results.

The mistake, with even a hint of dishonesty on the part of the leader, was saying that Evelyn was ready to meet the expectations of student leadership. If we agree that maturity and faithfulness to Christ are important characteristics for student leadership, we must also conclude that not every teenager is ready to move into such a role. It usually isn't wise to take on students who would be considered leadership "projects" unless you have a larger group or you feel like God truly is leading you this direction. Often, if a student is added who doesn't share the focus, desire, and even leadership skills of the other students, he or she will tend to thwart the unity and efforts of the group as a whole. Some students, like Evelyn, are better served by climbing some steps to maturity and "working" their way into student leadership. If you maintain high expectations, students will think the work is worth it.

Steppingstones

It's difficult to single out certain students for leadership. We're afraid to give the appearance that we've given up on students by saying no, especially those who might be close to being student leaders. Configuring the steps toward student leadership allows us opportunities to help them grow into their roles. As we interview students, we may discover any number of issues. They may care too much about what others think, or not enough about putting others first. Their ongoing walk with Christ may be anything but faithful. Perhaps their soft commitments have hindered their integrity with others.

Christ often ministered to people who others were trying to keep away or marginalize (Matthew 19:13-15; Luke 18:35-43; John 8:1-11). We should never give up on students just because they don't fit our student-leadership molds. Steppingstone opportunities give youth leaders extended influence in students' lives without jeopardizing the efforts and dynamics of the student leadership team.

Possible Steppingstones

• Regular meetings with an adult for three months to work on aspects of life where maturity and faithfulness to Christ need work

• Mission trips or service projects to demonstrate humility and servanthood

• Participation in a brief teaching role in some formal setting (Sunday school, small group, Bible study)

• Demonstration of consistent servanthood by helping set up or tear down for meetings or events

• Assignment to work on a specific behavior, such as sarcasm, over a period of time

• Reading through a particular book with a staff member

• Participation in various activities or outreach events

• A "waiting period" (a semester or even a year) just to spend time participating in the youth ministry

---

Staffing

One of the biggest practical implications of our research has to do with the need for involving other adults in the process of leading and coaching teenagers. While this issue has been pressed forcefully throughout the book, it may be helpful to think through the concrete steps required.

• Look for adults who exhibit the life you'd like students to emulate (evangelism lifestyle and ability, consistency in discipleship, prayer, maturity, faithfulness).

• Adults must be available to give time and energy to the students and not just attend the formal meeting times. Notes, calls, and appointments are all part of the relationship/coaching process.

• Adults must be able to "coach" students effectively. Listening, empathy, and a connection with students is important. If the students aren't interested in listening to or spending time with an adult, there is a problem.

• Structure the student-leadership team to facilitate adult coaching. Some youth ministries divided the larger student leadership group into smaller teams so each adult had a consistent group to focus time and energy on. The teams were centered on a school, re-volved around a small group, or were composed from a grade (such as freshmen or soph-omores) at school. The adults led and coached each of these teams, holding them ac-countable and helping the student leaders with their praying, inviting, and telling strategies.

The Activities of Student Leadership

Praying Practices—Lynn ran a West Coast youth ministry and was experiencing a personal richness in her own walk with Christ. The daily devotional times she had were in-spiring, and she desired that same inspiration for her students. Knowing prayer was vital, she wanted to find ways to increase the quality and frequency of students' prayer lives. She used a number of methods. First she created reminder cards for students to carry through-out the week. She also organized phone prayer chains for students to contact each other quickly when prayer was needed. Students were coached to organize regular (even daily) morning gatherings for prayer somewhere at school. Lynn taught on prayer regularly, mak-ing it an important part of their group times each week. The teenagers did meet daily for prayer, and many students still carry their prayer reminders (they were laminated) with them. The group is experiencing God in new ways now, and Lynn would tell you it started when she tended to the quality and frequency of prayer in her students' lives.

Inviting Ideas—It's first necessary to have specific events to invite others to attend. These can be either special events or regular meeting nights with a special "inviting" fo-cus. In the first case, you should determine the number of specific outreach events each school year you believe you can do at an acceptable level of quality for your teenagers. In the second case, regular meetings must still bear the standard of quality if they are to re-ally help student leaders in their ministry of inviting. There are a number of resources that can help you create and plan at a level of quality.

Most of the ministries in the research project did not innovate great new events with high non-Christian appeal in their approach to outreach. Rather they created an atmos-phere of expectancy regarding new people attending. Students welcomed others at the door. Student-leadership meetings provided a chance for students to monitor how well their group did at building positive emotional connections with others. Leaders frequently taught students how to reach out and pay attention to those who were new to the group. Each planning session for student leadership talked about whether meetings were "safe" socially and emotionally. The attention given to reaching out beyond common boundaries was a constant feature of the group.

Does your youth ministry operate with a lot of traditions, usually performing the same annual activities? Do your teenagers and staff tell a lot of "inside jokes" and huddle together at meetings? Do you overhear conversations in your group revealing a desire to minister to outsiders and new attendees? Do you hear reports of an internal drive in your students to invite their friends? These four questions serve as quick checkpoints to monitor the "inviting quotient" of your ministry.

Students in our study talked often to us about their groups' unity, acceptance, ability to forgive, understanding toward non-Christian teenagers, and safety. They were very aware of the reputations of their youth ministries at school, a critical bit of knowledge when it comes to evangelism. They knew what student conversation between classes, on the phone, at games and events sounded like in the community; they heard it through the grapevine. What the grapevine has to say about your youth ministry can be a fruitful ally or a poisonous weed if it turns against you.

As we stated in chapter 5, the confidence students have in your ministry plays an important role in their inviting habits. The grapevine can erode that confidence level. All the mailings, T-shirts, and school visits you can produce won't overcome a poor reputation among the student body. Students participate in that conversation from the moment they leave the activities of your youth ministry. Do you know what the grapevine is saying about your youth ministry? Is your desire to have an outreach ministry to your local schools hindered by the word on the street?

The character of your group will influence the grapevine as much or more than your activities. Paying attention to the emotional and social safety of your meetings will help ensure the grapevine conversations about your ministry are positive.

Telling Times—The chief characteristic of the youth ministries in this research project was their commitment to verbal evangelism. Most of the youth ministries structured regular evangelism training into their weekly schedule. More than just an occasional workshop or Wednesday-night topic, these groups had another hour or evening during the week when evangelism training took place. The training wasn't just a lecture or in a classroom, but they went out as a group and did it! These groups had focused witnessing efforts where everyone either shared their faith during a "Compelled to Tell" week or went out in teams to share with people at a mall, on the street, or in homes.

By making time to go out and share the gospel with others, groups value the actual practice of evangelism. Remember, adults set the pace for students. Modeling evangelism is fundamental to seeing teenagers share their faith with other teenagers. Make sure your students see adults and other students verbally share their faith on a regular basis.

Take Them Somewhere!

Effective youth ministry is no accident: Never assume it's going to happen. A renewed excitement and focus on student leadership in youth ministry dare not cause us to settle for a "measured" approach to this group. They have unlimited potential! If you've been careful in selection, you should be able to pour yourself freely into these students' lives as they desire to share their faith with their friends. One youth minister of a large group gives his leadership team unlimited 24/7 access to him.

It's also great to be proactive and take them somewhere. Bust past the barriers and the "big gulf" that keep us from experiencing God in new ways! Pray in earnest, and help your group be humble before God. So many of the student leaders in our study mentioned the life-changing impact of mission trips that we'd be wrong not to advocate this strategy. If you want to do a mission trip, do it well and go somewhere where God will stretch you.

Mission Trips With an Evangelism Focus

There are important factors to consider when organizing a mission trip with the express purpose of helping students better share their faith.

• Answer the question "What does God want us to do?" Can you step out of the door of your office and talk to your church board or students with confidence that a mission trip is what God desires for the youth ministry?

• Select a philosophy for the trip. What activities would you want to do on the trip? More than just a cross-cultural tour or work team, you should consider how you'll build into the trip a strong prayer emphasis and one-on-one opportunities for students to share the gospel. If you want to help your students learn to share their faith, they all should be ushered into situations where they tell others about Jesus on the trip.

• Prayerfully consider where you want to go. It might seem obvious, but it's important to ask, "Where are my students spiritually and developmentally? What cultural and geographical setting best helps our purposes and fits our group?" Trips within the country and to countries where there is no language barrier are good trips for first-timers. Unless you have a lot of trip experience or contacts, working with a mission organization geared toward leading youth trips is a blessing. They handle all the logistics and allow youth staff to relationally lead your students and reduce your stress load. Carefully select your organization, however, so you're comfortable with them theologically and philosophically, and you know they're committed to helping you move your students forward in prayer and in "telling" opportunities.

• Institute an application and screening process. Have students fill out applications for the trip and then go through a rigorous interview. It's not wise to take just anyone who wants to go, but you may sometimes take students who want to go just to watch and learn from the other students. That's acceptable on some trips. Be sure you keep in mind the philosophy you have chosen.

• Provide training. It certainly seems this is at least half the mission trip's influence in the lives of students. As they prepare for the trip and engage in spiritual disciplines, they experience God moving in their lives. There are many topics to cover that contribute to effective evangelism: being flexible in adverse circumstances, being able to share their faith at any moment, understanding the culture they are going to, and being dependent on the Holy Spirit as they take risks to share Christ. The team should begin meeting about six months before the trip to pray together, build a common team purpose, agree on team behavioral guidelines, learn about the culture and ministry ahead, and work on their ability to verbally share their faith.

When considering mission trips, it's important to be obedient to how you feel God is leading. These aren't magical events that painlessly transform your students into mature and faithful evangelists. But their track records are pretty impressive. They have a natural transformational power that—when accompanied by purposeful, quality training—can have an enormous, life-changing impact.

Seeing the world in a new way may help your group experience God in a new way. Constantly think about ways to stretch their understanding of God, and what God can do through them. Celebrate your progress and spotlight those students who emerge as models of effective and faithful student leaders. If you aren't praying, inviting, or telling as a group, redefine the student leadership's purpose and then go for it!

Personal Epilogue

The discoveries of this research project have had and continue to have significant personal impact on us as we really try to understand and integrate what we've learned. In this epilogue we will take turns sharing some of these personal reflections. We offer it as a last bit of encouragement to those who—like us—are still on the journey toward more faithful and effective ministry.

Dave

My first response to the findings from our research was fairly typical for me. I helped start P.I.T. training and input through the local Campus Life club where I volunteer. Kent Yost, our veteran full-time staff person, welcomed my input, and we did a nice job last year helping our more than fifty student leaders think of their most important roles as praying, inviting, and telling.

I also designed our Huntington College Student Leadership Training Experience around the findings in this book, believing that if kids went away from our weekend training strengthened in the Student Leader Three-Step, they'd be helped along their journey significantly. The feedback from students and staff has been affirming.

In fact, it was in preparation for teaching some of our insights to students attending the 1999 conference that I got blindsided by the Lord. I was looking for ways to hammer home the truth that you simply *can't pray too often,* or *with too many people* about evangelism matters if you really want to be effective at bringing people to Christ. I started thinking about the semester during high school when I saw a great number of my own friends come to Christ. That was the greatest period of fruitfulness I've ever seen in twenty-eight years of ministry! Then it hit me. I had never connected that remarkable experience with a parallel practice going on in my life at that time. I started each day during that semester in typing class with another Christian friend. We typed our prayers for the day (always ministry related) and exchanged them with one another so we could pray throughout the day.

It's the only time in my life I have had a discipline and structure helping me to pray virtually every day for God to use me in evangelism efforts with my friends.

It was the greatest period of evangelism effectiveness in my life.

I cried. I was so ashamed that it had taken me so long to see the connection as a *necessity!* I've always prayed and always been involved in evangelism, but my prayer life was never so concentrated on faithfully sharing my faith as it was at that time.

So I've made two immediate and personal adjustments. My son, Jason, is beginning his freshman year in high school. I have made it a point to pray with him every day about his evangelism efforts with his peers and the outreach opportunities in my life. We are praying specifically, like I used to when I was seventeen and good at this stuff. I have this discipline locked into my daily calendar on my computer to make sure I do it.

I'm determined to be an exception to the pattern of our research on at least one count. I will be a parent who models evangelism in front of my children.

Thank the Lord for that which helps us reflect deeply, bringing us—sometimes painfully—face to face with our need for change in the direction of faithfulness. The Bible has always been the number one tool God uses to "tune me up." It's nice to know he uses empirical research studies, too.

Terry

One of the most encouraging aspects of this project was discovering exciting ministries and youth workers who are faithful to God around the country. Whenever we would step off a plane, we were greeted by men and women serving God without a lot of recognition. They were reaching teenagers in their community and often they would report names of other youth ministries in their cities or towns who were enjoying similar richness in ministry. While their names never grace the headlines or they may never have led workshops at conventions, they are part of what God is doing around the country in communities and schools. It was encouraging to me, and I hope it is to you as you faithfully serve the One who's called you to this often discouraging and lonely avenue called youth ministry.

To be honest, student leadership had recently been somewhat of a struggle for me. After eight years of "successful" student leadership in Youth for Christ, that success has been a more elusive prey at the church where I am serving. The struggle has been wrestling with purpose, busyness of students, lack of student interest, and a definition of what student leadership looks like.

Having said that, the findings from the research have started a new safari for our local efforts at Hope Missionary. As our youth ministry—for three years in the peer-encouragement stage—moves across the "big gulf" this year, we are excited about what's ahead, anticipating a new stage of vitality in the student ministry here.

The story of how we got to this point centers on God and prayer. As I witnessed first-hand the way groups changed because of prayer and I saw the statistics directly parallel their prayer lives, I woke up. I no longer take it for granted that prayer and God's work in our group are automatics. Once we as a group started to truly pray, our trip across the "big gulf" began.

The second area I renewed my confidence in was the volunteer adult staff. While we've always had many adults, I tended to do a lot myself. We restructured our whole ministry to facilitate more adult/student coaching and modeling. While we still have steps to go here, we are seeing more students become more faithful because of this structural and philosophical change.

The third area where we changed immediately was in a group-wide effort to focus on the praying, inviting, and telling practices. We mention it almost weekly from up front, and we print it on various reminders so students can understand and hopefully emulate those values. We have more work to do in this area, but we are seeing students share their faith with other students now and work at developing a heart and life for evangelism.

It has been exciting to see the changes in the group as we've tended to different values. I wish I could say I've captured the student-leadership secret here, but it's still a work in progress. We've started over (and small) and will build slowly and with excellence. I hope your journey will be as rich and rewarding as mine has been.